The World of Pond Stories

Dr. Stewart Bitkoff

Abandoned Ladder

Copyright © 2018 by Stewart Bitkoff

goldpath@ptd.net

Except as permitted under U.S. Copyright Law, no part of this book may be reprinted, reproduced, transmitted, or utilized in any form by any electronic, mechanical, or other means, now known or hereafter invented, including photo-copying, microfilming, and recording, or in any information storage or retrieval system, without written permission from the publisher.

Printed in the United States of America

ISBN-13: 978-0-9915775-3-8

10 9 8 7 6 5 4 3 2 1

INTRODUCTION

The World of Pond is a special and magical place. The creatures that live here use their feelings and experiences to improve themselves and enjoy their lives.

Grasshoppers, dragon-flies, ants and turtles live in and around the water as neighbors and friends. Sure, there are disagreements, just like in our lives. Usually the animals talk to each other and easily work things out.

Young turtles attend silver minnow catching class. These classes teach turtles the discipline and skill required to catch different color minnows. This helps them learn to care for themselves and others. The brown and grey are easily caught, but the most difficult to catch and sweetest to eat is the silver minnow.

Turtle is a master of silver minnow catching and teacher of the young turtles. Besides showing young turtles how to catch minnows of all shapes and sizes, Turtle offers advanced students an opportunity to learn more about the silver minnow. In the movement of the silver minnow's tail, for example, a spiritual window of knowledge and understanding opens.

Before a young turtle can unlock the knowledge hidden in a silver minnow's tail, there is work to be done. The young turtles must learn about themselves and how to navigate through their thoughts and feelings. Often these thoughts and feelings block their awareness of the magical element and keep them from reaching a higher level of understanding about the meaning of life.

Contained in this collection are two books from The World of Pond series. The first book entitled *The World of Pond* is a group of 86 vignettes which are fable-like in presentation; the second book entitled *The Turtle Prophecy* follows Turtle as he goes on a mysterious spiritual quest and helps the mice of Berryville.

May you enjoy these stories and may they help you reach higher.

Dr. Stewart Bitkoff

Book I

The World of Pond

This work is for Lea, Holly, Melody,
And other young turtles
Who wish to catch silver minnows
With their mind.

-SB

Table of Contents

I Turtle & Grasshopper Stories 13

1. Eye on the Sky 15

2. Prayer or Coincidence? 17

3. Blind Faith 19

4. What is Lasting? 21

5. Smaller Death 23

6. When Are We Sleeping? 25

7. Lost Riches 27

8. Hope 29

9. Too Much of a Good Thing 31

10. Wanton Destruction 33

11. Help and Effort 35

12. Show-Off 37

13. All the Luck	39
14. Inner Peace	41
15. A Bad Thing	43
16. Hopes & Desires	45
17. The Right Way	47
18. Burning	48
19. Helping Others	50
20. Extraordinary Afternoon	55
21. The Capacity for Something	58
22. Self-Imposed Pressure	60
23. The Right Moment	62
24. Who Asked You?	63
25. Duty	65
26. The World-Famous Diver	67
27. Fame	71

28. The Guide Knows	73
29. Sensory Stimulation	74
30. Obsession	76
31. Charity	78
32. The Explanation	79

II Turtle Stories — 81

33. A Quiet Moment	83
34. Just A Dream	85
35. Missed Opportunity	87
36. Search	89
37. The Cycle	92
38. Larger View	94
39. Frightened of Self	96
40. All That Glitters	98
41. The Right Spot	100

42. Harmony 102

43. Deep Inside 104

44. Thinking About Himself 106

III Silver Minnow Catching Stories 109

45. Shocked Into Reality 111

46. Patterns 113

47. All the Facts 115

48. Stale Bread 117

49. The Proper Way 119

50. Hollow Words 121

51. One In a Hundred 123

52. Enough In It 125

53. Which Do You Want To Be? 127

54. Fix On The Goal 129

55. What's a Turtle For?	131
56. Following The Path	133
57. Well, Which Is It?	135
58. Why Try?	137
59. What The Teacher Knows	139
60. Wrong Time, Wrong Place, Wrong Turtles	141
61. Right Time, Right Place, Right Turtles	143
62. What Did You Do About It?	145

IV Young Turtle Stories   147

63. Pupils They Deserve	149
64. Filling The Emptiness	150
65. An Ancient Science	152
66. Reaching Completion	154
67. Strange Behavior	156

68. The Same Method — 158

69. Happiness — 159

70. Reaching A Minnow's Mind — 161

71. The Organization — 163

72. Young Turtle's Enlightenment — 165

V Meadow Stories — 167

73. Three Sisters — 169

74. When You Are Flying — 171

75. Emotional Reaction — 172

76. Three Ants on a Log — 174

77. Hand of Fate — 176

78. Be a Beetle — 178

79. Your Teacher's Words — 179

80. Snail's View — 181

81. Self-Importance — 182

82. Rotten Luck   183

83. Waiting Deep Within   184

84. A Second Chance   186

85. A Different View   188

86. Sylvester's Hiss   190

Dr. Stewart Bitkoff

I - Turtle & Grasshopper Stories

1. EYE ON THE SKY

One morning, Turtle was sitting beside the road and complaining about the sun's heat. "Feel how hot the sun is! Perhaps I should return to my burrow and wait until later in the day, when it is cooler, to search for flies."

Just then a Grasshopper came hip-hopping-along-singing this song:

> The sun is warm and the day is filled with Grace.
>
> The Great Hopper is in heaven and everything is in its Place.

When Grasshopper saw his friend, he stopped to talk. "Turtle isn't this a glorious day? Not a cloud in the sky and I am on my way to see my brother who lives in the distant meadow. Who could ask for more?"

Turtle replied, "Perhaps you like this weather but I am hot. I have this heavy shell to carry and I cannot move as easily as you."

Suddenly out of the sky a large crow swooped down, caught Grasshopper in its beak and carried him away.

Quickly, for a Turtle, that is, he turned around and scurried back to his burrow for safety. As Turtle scanned the sky to see if the crow was coming back for him, Turtle lamented, "Poor Grasshopper, I will miss him, but he got what he deserved; always trusting and never suspicious of others. He should have kept an eye on the sky!"

The Lesson

- Most often we blame our troubles on bad luck, other people or Deity/Karma. For every one life is a series of ups and downs.

- While it is a good idea to keep a look out for potential problems, we cannot become so concerned with bad things happening, that we miss opportunities to be joyful and spontaneous. Remember no matter who you are, one day life will jump up and bite you; this contrast balances with the more positive things that happen to us on a daily basis.

2. PRAYER OR COINCIDENCE?

Grasshopper was struggling to free himself from the crow's beak, moaning all the while, "Why me? Why do terrible things always happen to me? Surely I will live only a few more moments. If I had lived there were so many things I wanted to do."

Then Grasshopper offered up a prayer in the hope he would be saved. "Great Grasshopper, if you will save me, I promise to correct my bad habits and do whatever you want me to do. Surely I was not meant to die as take-out for some crow!"

Just then two crows who routinely made their living stealing from others, decided they wanted Grasshopper for themselves. So the crows attacked, and in defending himself, the first crow dropped Grasshopper. As Grasshopper fell to the ground, all three crows lost interest. The first crow had become angry and the two robber crows, now, had to protect themselves.

Luckily for Grasshopper, he fell uninjured into some tall grass and hid there until evening. Then he started to make his way back to tell everyone how his prayer was answered, and he was saved by the Great Grasshopper.

The Lesson

- Often in life there is a hidden dimension to outcomes and events. The workings of the unseen world are mysterious and known only to a few.

- Was Grasshopper saved by the workings of the Unseen Forces or is it just business as usual for the robber crows? They routinely patrol the meadow sky looking to steal another bird's food; and Grasshopper benefited from their raid.

- Was this the hand of fate? Or simply coincidence? Dear reader, ultimately this is something you must decide; Grasshopper feels he was favored by his God. At any rate, which ever you decide, divine intervention or coincidence; for me it is too early in the game to kill off one of the main characters in The World of Pond.

3. BLIND FAITH

The next morning, Grasshopper arrived at Turtle's burrow and called inside. "Turtle, are you there? This is Grasshopper. I am safe and have a wonderful story to tell about how the Great Grasshopper saved me from a crow. Are you inside?"

"Grasshopper is that really you? I thought that I would never see you again. I'm so happy you're safe but I have no time for stories right now. I am waiting for a fly to fly into my burrow so I can catch it and have breakfast. Come back later when I am not so busy."

"Turtle, you know that a fly will not enter your burrow when you are there. They can sense your presence and do not want to be eaten."

"Grasshopper you have no faith. Didn't your God just save you from a crow? I am sure my God can send me breakfast."

The Lesson

- All of us believe what we are doing at the moment is the most important thing, sometimes overlooking the need to be flexible and caring with those we love.

- Also, we see events in a pattern that fits our needs, and may be unable to accept we are not seeing events clearly. We may not understand that we use our own filters automatically, and sometimes those filters need an adjustment.

- Turtle reasons, if the Great Grasshopper just saved Grasshopper, why wouldn't the Great Turtle send him breakfast? Surely his God is equally capable?

- Clearly Turtle is not seeing events as they are; a fly will not enter while Turtle is there, but Turtle has convinced himself otherwise.

4. WHAT IS LASTING?

Turtle had been preparing all day for his dinner honoring Grasshopper. Turtle got up early and picked grass from the meadow and by the pond. He found six different varieties and brought fresh water from the spring.

Turtle cleaned all afternoon readying his burrow for the festive occasion. Turtle wanted to hear in detail the story of Grasshopper's escape from the crow. Feeling badly about his insensitivity on the morning of Grasshopper's return, Turtle wanted to make it up to Grasshopper by planning a celebration dinner.

Turtle caught some mayflies and silver minnows for himself. Working for hours, Turtle eagerly anticipated the evening's fun. When Grasshopper arrived the two friends sat down and began to eat and talk. In less time than you can say, "I'm hungry," Grasshopper finished all six of the grasses and was sipping the spring water. Grasshopper fasted all day in anticipation and ate quickly due to his enormous hunger.

Turtle, a little disappointed, thought to himself. "Gee, I worked so hard preparing this dinner. In a matter of moments, the food was gone. Was it really worth all the effort?"

At that moment Grasshopper was thinking, "I am so happy to be sitting here with my friend. The memory of Turtle's kindness will always stay with me. The food was good but the friendship is better."

And as the evening proceeded, both friends shared each other's company and the evening was a complete success.

The Lesson

- Reality is often perceived differently by each individual. These views combine to form the larger view of life.

- Often in life anticipated events are over in "the gulp of six grasses." That is why the wise tell us to enjoy the journey; or in this case for Turtle the preparation and good feelings that surround getting ready.

5. SMALLER DEATH

Turtle was asleep and dreaming of climbing a steep hill with a large rock tied to his leg.

After a time he fell down, exhausted from the climb. As he lay sweating and fatigued, Turtle heard his inner voice call out: "While everyone must face physical death, of greater value is the death which precedes it. This death is the smaller death and the goal of your long seeking."

In the morning when Turtle awoke, somehow, he felt happier. When he got up to go find breakfast, he noticed there was a large rope lying beside his bed. With lighter steps, Turtle set about the tasks of the day.

The Lesson

- Somehow during his sleep, Turtle's higher consciousness provided an answer to his mysterious behavior of dragging a large rock around on a heavy rope.

- For spiritual travelers, it is said that much of the Teaching occurs at night while we are sleeping. For scientists, what goes on while we are sleeping is still pretty much a mystery.

Ask yourself where do you go when you are asleep? Besides those jumbled dreams what else is going on?

- Turtle experiences the smaller death; death of self, while he is sleeping. In his dream he is set free, in a sense, from worldly duties; which are represented by rope and rock. Thus he becomes freer to travel spiritually.

6. WHEN ARE WE SLEEPING?

Later in the morning, Turtle sought out Grasshopper to tell him about the dream. After hearing the story of the rope coming undone, Grasshopper didn't know quite what to make of it.

"Turtle, I have heard of things like this happening in dreams. But are you sure that you didn't untie the rope yourself? Perhaps it came undone by twisting in your sleep?

"Grasshopper, I cannot tell you for sure what happened. It was unlike any dream that I have ever had. For a time it seemed as if I was awake in my dream and my normal life was the life of sleep. Now, I no longer know which is real.

"This morning I see everything in a different light. Everything is part of a greater reality and joined in the Light of Truth. It is as if I am seeing the world through new eyes and for the first time."

The Lesson

- Now Turtle realizes that in some ways the next world is more real or lasting than this world.

The World of Pond Stories

- In his sleep, Turtle experienced the world of spirit which underlies all things; this has caused him to become a little unsettled, viewing daily life differently.

7. LOST RICHES

Grasshopper was watching the south meadow being consumed by a swarm of locusts. This made him terribly distraught.

Later in the day, Turtle inquired, "Why are you so upset? There is plenty of grass to go around. After all, the east and north meadow are rarely touched by the locusts."

"I didn't tell you? My grandfather made me heir to the south meadow. I found out about my inheritance about a week ago. Now there is nothing left."

"Cheer up at least you were rich for week and knew the joy of being wealthy. That's more than most. Think positive, the grass may eventually grow back."

The Lesson

- Attachment to things, people, thoughts and outcomes can slow the traveler down. It is said that he who travels lightly has the best chance of reaching the goal. The wise claim all we can take with us to the next place is the love in our hearts.

- Turtle points out to Grasshopper that all riches/attachments are transitory; even if they last for years. Also, Turtle reminds Grasshopper at least he was wealthy for a week and had these good feelings.

8. HOPE

Grasshopper was hopping through the south meadow. It was desolate. The locusts had chewed on everything. Not a flower, not a blade of grass or vine was left untouched.

Amidst the devastation, Grasshopper sat down and started to cry. As he sobbed, he looked down at the ground, and lo and behold, a small blade of grass was struggling to emerge from the dirt. Quickly Grasshopper cleared away the rubble, and hidden from the locusts was a small, green, thatch of grass.

At this sight, Grasshopper offered a prayer of thanks to the Great Hopper, and felt everything would be alright.

The Lesson

- Amidst the storm and struggle, when a ray of sunshine appears, our hearts gladden. In the darkness of the long night, it is easy to forget morning will follow; both are part of a cycle.

- This story reminds us all, as Grasshopper cleared away the rubble and found some grass, one day joy will replace sorrow. That is the natural order.

9. TOO MUCH OF A GOOD THING

Turtle was eating one grape after another. When Grasshopper came hopping by Turtle had been doing this for most of the morning.

Grasshopper looked at Turtle and could see that he was turning purple. Alarmed, Grasshopper questioned Turtle about his behavior.

"Grasshopper, I figure it this way. One grape is said to have the wisdom of the cosmos contained in it so if I eat 100 grapes then I will have the knowledge of a 100 universes in my system."

At this point, Turtle passed out. Not fully understanding Turtle's logic, Grasshopper shook his head in confusion, then continued on his way.

The Lesson

- We all have a need to get things done quickly; this stems from greed and an assumption that we always know what we need and can prescribe for any situation.

- On a spiritual journey, many travelers randomly consume books, prayers and lectures like they are the grapes of this story; hoping to digest and make use of them as quickly as possible.

- In all things a balance is required. Here Turtle learns this lesson in a most uncomfortable way; passing out from eating too much and too quickly.

10. WANTON DESTRUCTION

A young turtle came rushing, for a turtle, that is, to Grasshopper and exclaimed "Come quickly, come quickly, Turtle is acting very strange. He is catching minnow after minnow, throwing them in a hole and not letting anyone eat them. He is just killing them for what looks like the fun of it."

Quickly Grasshopper hopped down to the pond and sure enough there was a pile of minnows squirming around in a large hole. Nearby Turtle was working furiously to catch more minnows and not letting anyone near them. A large crowd of young turtles had gathered. Everyone was outraged and bewildered by Turtle's behavior.

Out of the corner of his eye, Turtle saw Grasshopper and yelled, "Do not interfere! If you try to stop me I will bite off your head. Stand back!"

Turtle continued catching minnows for hours and no one interfered. Everyone was frightened. Finally, Turtle stopped, exhausted. Grasshopper ventured closer and inquired, "Friend, you acted like a turtle possessed today. I cannot believe you would kill all these minnows for no reason. Surely there must have been a reason. Why?"

Turtle paused for a moment and replied, "To some this appeared irresponsible and useless. To others who know they will see the purpose. These minnows are diseased, and they must be destroyed or they would have infected the entire pond."

The Lesson

- When someone is working often there is no time for an explanation. There is a job to be done and to take the time to explain could interfere or delay the outcome.

- In this situation, time was critical and Turtle was working on a higher level. He had information and insight that others did not have; if an explanation was offered it could jeopardize outcome. And because an explanation that others could understand was unavailable, the citizens of pond considered Turtle mad/crazy.

- According to tradition, there are servants working in this world, unseen, and if viewed by others, would be considered 'crazy;' unless precious time was taken to explain. And if these hidden servants were to explain, most would not even believe the reason for their behavior.

11. HELP AND EFFORT

Somehow Turtle had rolled onto his back and was having a terrible time trying to flip back over. Turtle was lying this way for hours and feared he had reached the end of his days. Everyone knows it is impossible for a turtle to right himself.

So Turtle lay in the road, sobbing. Suddenly along came Grasshopper and sensing the urgency of the situation inquired, "Turtle what has happened to you? Don't you know if you don't turn over, eventually, you will die?"

"Grasshopper, I am doomed. Turtles cannot turn themselves over. It is a law of nature."

"This is terrible! Terrible! Let me think. After a few moments, Grasshopper inquired, "Have you tried to turn over?"

"Well... no. What's the point? Everyone knows it is impossible."

"Come on then. Perhaps if you start rocking and I help a little, we can get you over."

Turtle started rocking back and forth. After a few moments, Turtle gained momentum and began to rock faster and faster. At just the right moment, Grasshopper gave a quick kick and Turtle flipped over.

Then, Turtle and Grasshopper went on their way.

The Lesson

- Often we are imprisoned and limited by our own thoughts. Some of this is based upon social beliefs and some by our own evaluation of the situation.

- What may be required to get past this sticking point is a different view of what is possible. Sometimes this different view is offered by friends, family or a good teacher.

- For the spiritual traveler, this alternate view is offered through intuitive or spiritual knowledge.

- Turtle represents rational thought which is often the ordinary way of approaching a problem; while Grasshopper represents intuitive knowledge that is useful in the world.

12. SHOW-OFF

Grasshopper felt proud of helping Turtle in his hour of need. Full of glee and self-importance, Grasshopper twirled around before the other hoppers singing:

> Look at me, look at me,
>
> I'm as happy as can be.
>
> I've helped a friend
>
> In his hour of distress.
>
> As far as friends go,
>
> I'm the best...

Then Grasshopper slipped on a wet leaf and fell to the ground. Instead of getting right up and continuing his dance, Grasshopper clutched at his leg, more embarrassed than injured, and moaned:

"Why does something bad always happen to me? Things were going along so well. Now my happiness is ruined."

The Lesson

- In a troubling situation, most often we look to Karma or the mysterious Hand of Fate; yet usually it is our effort which sets in motion a series of events. Good events are always followed by bad ones; that is the universal law of opposites. Also in our affairs many times we look for and ascribe divine intervention; when it really is natural laws at work.

- Grasshopper should have been a little more observant and aware of his environment. Noting the leaves were wet, he could have tempered his celebrating and not jumped as high or moved to a drier location.

13. ALL THE LUCK

Grasshopper was happily hopping along the road, when he tripped over a stone. Lying on the ground, holding his bruised leg, Grasshopper was in great pain. As he lay motionless, dazed by the fall, along came another hopper. Effortlessly this fellow avoided the stone and continued on his journey, unaware of Grasshopper's plight.

Grasshopper thought, "Some hoppers have all the luck. Things come so easily to them."

After a time, Grasshopper got up and began to limp home. When he turned the bend in the road, he was shocked to find the other hopper squashed beneath a fallen branch.

Obviously dead for a short time, Grasshopper exclaimed, "My goodness that could have been me. Some hoppers have all the luck."

The Lesson

- We have presented two views of life events. Initially Grasshopper sees his fall on the stone as a matter of bad luck. Yet if he looked more closely it was probably due to inattentiveness on the road.

- Later when Grasshopper meets up with the second hopper, who missed the stone, only to have a more serious accident, Grasshopper again explains this event as bad luck.

- In both instances, Grasshopper missed other possible factors that could have contributed to the events. His fall could have been due to inattentiveness as well as the location of a potentially dangerous stone; and the second hopper's accident could have been affected by those factors or, simply, destiny.

- For the spiritual traveler, all of these factors: luck, personal effort and destiny are potentials of the situation. Further what some call luck, others call Karma, and only the Wise, through Higher Consciousness, know the Truth for sure.

14. INNER PEACE

Grasshopper was seated beside the road hidden between rocks. As Turtle approached he noticed Grasshopper was sitting in a strange position with his eyes closed. Turtle became curious and inquired, "Grasshopper, what are you doing?"

Grasshopper replied, "Be still Turtle. Can't you see that I am meditating? I need complete silence."

"Meditating... what's that?"

"Oh Turtle don't you know anything? I am trying to reach inner peace by closing my eyes to the world and stilling all my inner fears and desires."

Turtle thought for a moment then exclaimed, "Now I get it. You reach inner peace by closing your eyes because that makes all the crows go away!"

The Lesson

- Many travelers believe there is a one step, fix-it-all technique to the ups and downs of life. Grasshopper uses the technique of meditation to try and quiet his fears and reach lasting inner peace.

- Grasshopper is unaware that inner peace is transitory; one moment we are at peace and happy: then something happens, and we lose our balance, only to start all over again.

- Turtle, unfamiliar with meditation and spiritual learning, tries to explain Grasshopper's quest in the only way he can. In a hopper's world, crows are the biggest fear and by closing his eyes, Grasshopper rids himself of them; because he cannot see them.

15. A BAD THING

Worried, Turtle was seated beside Grasshopper. Grasshopper had been semi-conscious for three days, refusing all liquids and grasses. Miraculously he hadn't died from the high fever or dehydration.

Just before this illness struck, Turtle recalled how strangely Grasshopper had acted. Grasshopper had been eating and drinking continuously for days. At first Turtle thought it was this strange behavior which had caused the illness. Later Turtle realized if Grasshopper hadn't gone on a binge, he may have died from the fever. All of the seemingly excessive eating and drinking of the previous days had offered protection for Grasshopper.

Sometimes a bad thing can be good.

The Lesson

- Many times in life, events occur and we have no explanation for them. In hindsight, we look back and realize these events were a preparation for something which followed.

- Here Grasshopper over-ate and drank excessively; unaware that he was storing nutrients to help with a fever his body was fighting and hadn't completely matured.

- For the spiritual traveler, sometimes in disappointment, they turn away from a path so that in the future they can embrace another that works better for them.

16. HOPES & DESIRES

Turtle was very, very slowly, dragging around a large rock that was tied with rope to his leg. When Grasshopper approached, Turtle was sweating and breathing heavily; he had been doing this for hours. Puzzled Grasshopper called out, "Friend what are you doing dragging that rock around. You are slow as molasses anyway; with that extra weight, surely you will never get any place on time. You might even get sick from all the exertion. Why don't you just untie the rope?"

Turtle replied, "This rock represents my hopes and desires. I am waiting for one of the perfected ones to cut the rope with the scissor of Truth. Until then, I am at the rock's mercy and must continue on in this fashion."

At this response, Grasshopper just shook his head and went on his way.

The Lesson

- In this action teaching, Turtle represents all of the pond creatures. While hopes and desires are an essential aspect to joyful, healthy living; when we hope too much or desire too much, we can lose our inner balance. Particularly when hopes and desires are not met; often we become disappointed and the emotional sting can temporarily block us from moving further along.

- Sometimes we are helped when someone we respect or a teacher points this out to us. Hoping for something beyond a certain point, in our future, in a spiritual search can be severely limiting, and needs to be cut loose like Turtle's rock.

- Then we can continue on our journey, traveling inward, without the "inner noise" of strong emotions.

- Because Grasshopper has not learned to shift his frame of reference to potential limiting factors on a spiritual journey, he does not understand what Turtle is teaching.

17. THE RIGHT WAY

Turtle was thrashing about in the pond and splashing water higher and higher into the air. Grasshopper called out, "Turtle what are you doing? You can't swim about like that for very long; soon you'll get tired!"

Turtle called back, "I'm not swimming. I'm trying to catch flies!"

Grasshopper laughed, calling back, "How can you catch flies splashing water high into the air? Don't you know it isn't done that way?"

Turtle replied, "It doesn't matter what you think; it's what the fly thinks that is important."

The Lesson

- Many times, we are imprisoned by our thoughts and the way we are taught to look at things (solve problems). Often the person who thinks outside the box- is considered a madman.

- Turtle is showing Grasshopper, there are many ways to solve a problem (catching flies); clearly as in this case some ways are better than others.

18. BURNING

It was the middle of the night and Turtle was tossing branches onto a bonfire outside his burrow. The flames were growing higher and brighter. All the while Turtle was yelling, "Burning, burning. What the Great Turtle desires is burning!"

Excitedly, Grasshopper asked Turtle, "What are you doing?"

Turtle replied, "How else may Truth be revealed but through burning. Truth cannot be seen in the darkness and only the soul that is ablaze with its own Light can realize it."

Young turtle asked Grasshopper, "What does Turtle mean by all this?"

Grasshopper said, "I don't have any idea."

The Lesson

- In this action teaching, Turtle tries to show young turtle and Grasshopper the intensity of love required to reach journey's end. To reach the Beloved, the traveler's heart and soul must be aflame with love. Each branch tossed on the fire, represents an action taken for God/Absolute; and as the fire grows stronger, consuming the different branches, the inner darkness is aglow with the burning Love and Light of Union.

- While action toward the Beloved is essential, an overlaying aspect of the spiritual journey is the Beloved's action toward the traveler. Two of the great Servants of God have said: "Love is not earned it is bestowed," and "God remembered me, long before I remembered Him; and came looking for me, long before I went looking for Him." Often it is this action by God/Absolute that tips the balance in favor of the lover.

- The traveler, who reaches journey's end, must be like the moth who desires only to be consumed by the candle's light.

19. HELPING OTHERS

Grasshopper was sad and feeling sorry for himself. He thought no one liked him and when it came to picking grasses, he didn't think he was as good as the other hoppers. He felt that all he ever got were the leftovers.

Grasshopper spent half the morning sitting beside the road worrying about what a terrible life he had. Then along came Turtle. Turtle could tell in an instant what Grasshopper's problem was and how to solve it.

Turtle called out, "If you're tired of feeling blue, follow me and I'll show you what to do!"

Grasshopper thought to himself, "Here's Turtle sticking his shell into my business again. But what have I to lose? I just can't shake these blues."

At Turtle's direction, the two friends began walking toward the meadow. Grasshopper had promised to do whatever Turtle said and not complain.

The meadow was alive with all kinds of creatures. Butterflies were flying. Bees were buzzing. Ants were crawling. What a wondrous sight to behold!

But these things just made Grasshopper sadder. Everyone was enjoying themselves and had something important to do except him.

After a time, Turtle and Grasshopper came upon a young hopper who was having a difficult time chewing through grasses and stacking them in a pack. One of the first lessons a young hopper learns is to identify six meadow grasses, stack them and bring them to his teacher.

As Turtle and Grasshopper continued to observe, the young fellow realized he was being watched. Without hesitation, he turned to Grasshopper and asked, "Will you help me?" Turtle nodded and in an instant Grasshopper was showing the young one how to identify, quickly chew through and stack grass.

In five minutes time, the young one had stacked his pack, thanked Grasshopper and was on his way to see his teacher.

As Turtle and Grasshopper continued walking, Grasshopper felt a little better. Somehow by helping another, his blues were turned into smiles. Turtle saw this and said, "We are not done yet."

The two friends continued on. Rounding a bend in the road, Turtle and Grasshopper came upon some ants who were struggling to free one of their brothers. A branch had fallen and trapped him beneath a small limb. The branch was heavy and the ants were having a terrible time with it.

Without hesitation, Turtle and Grasshopper helped the ants lift. Quickly, the injured fellow was pulled from beneath the limb. While he was being nursed and carried off by the others, the leader thanked Turtle and Grasshopper for their help.

By this time Grasshopper was hopping. He never felt better. He even began to sing. His sadness was completely gone.

Turtle looked at Grasshopper and said, "We are not done yet."

Grasshopper wondered what Turtle was up to next. Grasshopper was happy. "What else was there," he wondered.

Turtle and Grasshopper continued walking for about an hour. Turtle walked very slowly and this got on Grasshopper's nerves. Grasshopper felt like hopping, and if he knew where they were going, he could get there lickety-split. But no, Turtle wouldn't tell Grasshopper anything. Everything with Turtle was always a mystery and Grasshopper had promised to do whatever Turtle said without complaining.

They came to a stream. Turtle told Grasshopper to lift some stones and make a path into the water with them. Every few inches or so Turtle and Grasshopper placed another stone. They must have laid out a dozen or so.

In the hot sun, this work took about two hours. Grasshopper saw no point in what they were doing. Who would benefit from this path, which seemed to go nowhere? It only went part of the way across the stream.

At one point, Grasshopper was very frustrated and about to ask Turtle what was the reason for this work, when Turtle remarked, "No questions until tonight."

Finally, they finished. As the two walked back toward Pond, Grasshopper was hot, tired and angry. He didn't know why they worked so hard and couldn't wait to give Turtle a piece of his mind.

The Lesson

That evening after dinner, as Turtle and Grasshopper sat outside Turtle's burrow, he started to explain.

- "Often when we are feeling sorry for ourselves, it is best to find something to do. Activity is a cure for sadness. The best activity is to help another. This takes us out of ourselves and the helping energy is curative.

- "Helping others, like the young hopper, is part of our social duty and is part of life in Pond. Yet it is better to help before help is requested. This is the higher activity. Less indebtedness is created. Hence, we helped the ants before they could ask.

- Finally, a higher form of helping is when the one receiving help is unaware of the source. We placed those stones so young turtles could stand on them and catch silver minnows. They will think they are lucky to find this spot; never knowing what we did. Yet our energy is connected to this work and we benefit from it."

As Grasshopper watched the night sky, he was at peace. He was not sad. In fact, he never felt better. He realized, when we help others, we help ourselves.

Slowly he was beginning to understand.

20. EXTRAORDINARY AFTERNOON

It was a warm, sunny afternoon. The trees were beginning to change colors. The leaves were turning different shades of red, yellow, orange and green. The morning damp coolness had turned to dry warmth. Slowly summer was giving way to fall and all creatures knew that winter was soon approaching.

Feeling the gentle breeze as it blew across Pond, Grasshopper and Turtle rested in the brilliant sunshine. Grasshopper was beginning to fall asleep when Turtle called out, "Let's go for a walk." This was the last thing Grasshopper wanted. Turtle walked so slow; however, Grasshopper grudgingly agreed.

As the two friends walked beside the Pond, Turtle began to point things out to Grasshopper. "See how the young turtle has grey minnows to catch. Watch how he struggles to capture a snack. There, he has one now. Look over on that tree see the mother robin as she feeds her young an earthworm. Look how the young ones open to accept the gift of life."

Walking on further, Grasshopper wondered if Turtle had lost his mind. Why was he pointing out the commonplace activities and making such a big deal about it?

Next Turtle pointed to some bees as they flitted about the flowers. "Look, see how they gather the nectar to make honey. Moving from flower to flower, they help pollinate and provide an essential service to the meadow. Look over there. See the ants as they carry crumbs from the fallen crab apple. The Light is always providing."

By this time, Grasshopper was bored and had had enough of this walk, and said to Turtle, "I will meet you back at the burrow."

Hopping back to Turtle's burrow, Grasshopper wondered what this all had been about. It was a beautiful, fall afternoon, but why the need to point out the obvious? All these things happened every day. Sometimes, Grasshopper just couldn't understand what his friend was talking about.

The Lesson

- Later that evening, as the two friends rested in Turtle's burrow, Turtle began to explain. "You see, sometimes lessons occur in daily life. When the traveler is in tune, the commonplace becomes extraordinary. The Light is always providing for our needs. As the warm sunlight gives life to the Pond, so, the Light of Eternity gives substance to our soul. Just as there is food for our body, so, there is nourishment for the soul.

- The spiritual traveler must learn to see past everyday events and look for the pattern. The Light is forever loving and giving, as was this glorious afternoon. Without the Light, the world of forms would cease to exist."

- In amazement Grasshopper just shook his head. Clearly he had missed this opportunity to grow closer. However, he was grateful to have a friend who could help point out the subtle wonders of life.

- Truly this afternoon had been bathed in the Light of Eternity and, now, would stay forever in Grasshopper's mind.

21. THE CAPACITY FOR SOMETHING

Grasshopper reached the end of his rope. Everything he tried to do came up empty. He tried a business of his own selling meadow grass tea and not one package was sold. All the other hoppers claimed they could pick their own grass; all Grasshopper did was put a rubber band around a clump of grass. He studied spiritual matters with Swami Grassy Hoppah and nothing happened. In fact, he nearly died during his ten day fast for enlightenment. He forgot to drink enough fluids.

During his fitness period, all Grasshopper got for his effort were sore legs and joints. When he studied psychology and assertiveness training, Grasshopper never gave others a chance to talk and nearly became a social outcast around the Pond.

Grasshopper continued staring in the mirror and wondered what he could do to make progress? He was so mad.

Poor Grasshopper, he never realized there is a vast difference between the desire for something and the capacity for it. If Grasshopper would have stuck to being himself, a Grasshopper; perhaps he might have been more content?

The Lesson

- During the course of each life, the search for self-awareness is both internal and external.

- Often travelers go on various life journeys, filled with expectation of excitement and success; forgetting to travel inward as well.

- Inside there is a quiet whisper that will tell you who you are; you are multi-level and complex; filled with skills and capacity to become, "Whatever you wish." Sadly, sometimes we wish for the wrong thing.

- Remember, listen to that inner whisper, this voice will set you free and you will become your inner most desire.

22. SELF-IMPOSED PRESSURE

Grasshopper was hopping up and down. Jumping as high and as often as he could, yelling at the top of his lungs, "I'm going crazy! I'm going crazy! I just can't stand it anymore. My cousin wants me to meet her friend. My bills are past due. I need a vacation and my head aches. When will all this pressure end? I'm going crazy! I'm going crazy! I just can't stand it anymore!"

Grasshopper continued on in this fashion for hours. Remember grasshoppers are really good jumpers. Finally after one of his very high leaps, he hit his head on a branch and could no longer remember what he was so upset about.

The Lesson

- All of us have those days when we cannot stop our mind from jumping from one worry to another. This is our fear response running wild.

- Many times, the counter to this fear and worry cycle is switching attention or changing the station that we are listening too in our head. This change in thought is represented by the smack to the head Grasshopper received.

- In most situations, we can switch our attention through thought or activity: do something we enjoy, think a positive thought, say a prayer, or get up and do something for another. Sometimes we may have to repeat this activity to break the worry cycle.

- If none of these substitution devices work, get up take a long, hot shower and while showering, ask the Universe to free you from your worry for a time. Then do something positive for another person.

- Finally if you cannot break the worry cycle with a substitute activity, it may be time to take action of another sort. In Grasshopper's case it may be time to tackle his worry list: figure out how to pay those bills, plan a fun vacation, or tell his cousin he doesn't want to meet her friend.

23. THE RIGHT MOMENT

Grasshopper fell into the pond; unable to swim, he was thrashing about wildly, and calling out for help. Just as Grasshopper was going down for the third and last time, Turtle jumped in to rescue him.

Later when Grasshopper questioned Turtle why he waited so long to pull him out of the water, Turtle replied, "Until that moment you were just struggling. I jumped in when you really needed help and were drowning!"

The Lesson

- Here we see the difference between struggling and drowning/failing. There is a big difference.

- Everyone struggles and it is a much more dire situation when we are about to drown or completely fail.

- Through our struggles we may learn and grow stronger. When we fail there is less to discuss; however there may be much to think about.

24. WHO ASKED YOU?

Turtle was having a difficult time removing some dirt that had fallen in front of his burrow entrance. He had been at it all morning with little success, when Grasshopper came by. Sensing Turtle's difficulty removing the dirt, Grasshopper just naturally started to help.

After a time Grasshopper was working so hard that he didn't even notice Turtle's reluctance to continue with the task. He seemed to have lost interest.

Finally when the job was done, Turtle thanked Grasshopper while mumbling to himself, "Who does he think he is anyhow? Nobody even asked for his help. He just took the whole thing over."

And as Grasshopper started home he wondered, "What would Turtle have done without me? I bet he never would have gotten the job done. I wish he would have tried a little harder."

The Lesson

- Before starting, the helper must be aware of the recipient's attitude toward being helped. We must remember to ask if the person, or in this case Turtle, wants our help.

- Often we automatically assume when someone is struggling or in a difficult life situation, they want and will be grateful for assistance.

- As you can see, that is not always the case; sometimes an altruistic effort can be met with resentment and resistance.

- Particularly when the recipient's pride is hurt because we did not ask and respect his right to accept or deny. For some of us, accepting help is a sign of weakness.

25. DUTY

Grasshopper was reading a note card which his spiritual teacher had given him. He couldn't understand the applicability to his own life and gazed at it questioningly. It read: "Happiness and inner peace are byproducts. Higher knowledge is other than this."

Grasshopper remained confused about this statement for hours. Finally, he decided to set about his daily chores. After all there was work to be done. Unknowingly, by getting back to everyday activity, Grasshopper learned something about higher knowledge.

The Lesson

- Many spiritual travelers seek higher knowledge and spiritual learning because they desire happiness and inner peace. Yet, in some spiritual schools these two states are considered transitory, they come and go, depending upon circumstances.

- Grasshopper uses his spiritual energy to accomplish his daily tasks instead of unfruitfully trying to figure out the riddle on his teacher's note card.

- In authentic schools, spiritual learning and experience is offered so this learning can be of practical use in the world; going about the task of living our lives.

26. THE WORLD-FAMOUS DIVER

"Aha!" Finally, the light went on in Turtle's head. "Now I know what to do. I will become a World-Famous Diver. Then everyone will know my name. Let me see, how should I start? Perhaps I should get myself a diving instructor or read some books on the subject. No! That will take too long. I have a better idea."

So Turtle set about making some posters and placing them on trees in the meadow, along the road and by the Pond. Each poster read in large green and red letters: Come One, Come All, See the World Famous Diver, Wednesday 10 am, Brook Pond, No Admission Charge!

When the appointed hour arrived, a large crowd gathered; water bugs, turtles, minnows, grasshoppers, hedge hogs and snakes were all in attendance. None of the Pond creatures had ever seen a World-Famous Diver and every one was curious. Out of shiny material, Turtle made himself a red mask and a green cape; wearing his costume proudly, he slowly swam out to the large rock in the middle of the Pond and everyone cheered in anticipation. Slowly when Turtle climbed the rock, everyone sighed and took a deep breath.

Shocked when Turtle leaped head- first off the rock, everyone screamed.

Since Turtle had not taken into account the distance of the dive in relation to the depth of the water, Turtle smacked his head on the Pond bottom, rendering himself unconscious. And because no one knew what a World-Famous Diver was supposed to do, no one jumped in to see if Turtle was alright. Everyone assumed disappearing was part of the act and cheered, wildly, when he did not surface.

Fortunately, turtles can submerge and stay alive for long periods beneath the water; even when they smack their heads. When Turtle awoke and swam out of the Pond, no one was there to congratulate him.

Later when Turtle tried to explain to Grasshopper and the others, by showing his costume, he was The World-Famous Diver; they all laughed and said he shouldn't try to take credit for someone else's effort. Besides they pointed out, anyone could make himself a costume, but it took years of practice and considerable skill to become a World-Famous Diver.

The Lesson

- Often our human need for personal attention is deeply hidden and pushes us to do all kinds of things. This need is part of our primary need for love. Each traveler requires a balance of personal recognition, love and social interaction; this is necessary for healthy living.

- Many times our need for attention becomes attached to our spiritual journey, and when this occurs it manifests as a desire to be recognized for our spiritual knowledge and accomplishment; we may begin to teach or seek to be the favorite of our teacher; we may wear exotic garb and colorful costumes to be recognized for our affinity with this "more spiritual" way of life. Also we may write papers, blogs and books; all this activity in the name of sharing and helping others.

- Here Turtle plays the role of fool, seeking fame and fortune (attention); in order to get noticed, he adorns a colorful costume, performs a brave yet stupid act. Because he was not adequately prepared, he fell short of his mark, knocked himself out and no one believed him.

- In our quest for higher knowledge, many things must be in place before the inner wisdom comes forward.

- Part of preparation for higher knowledge, requires knowing when our need for personal attention: masquerades as something else.

- Often our hidden need for attention blocks any real spiritual progress.

27. FAME

One day, Grasshopper began thinking about Turtle's attempt to become a world-famous diver. Grasshopper too had grown tired of his everyday life and hatched a plan to change things. So he put up signs which read:

> Grasshopper the Extraordinary
> Reads the Future – Counselor to the Stars
> South Meadow – 8am-4pm Daily

Turtle happened by and seeing the signs inquired, "Grasshopper, why are you doing this? You're not a clairvoyant! What if everyone starts coming to you for advice? Didn't you learn anything from my diving fiasco?"

"Oh, I know I'm not clairvoyant, but they don't. Besides if someone comes to see me I'll give them some general advice, ask for a donation and tell them to come back in a month or two. What's important is that everyone thinks I have extraordinary powers. Actually, I don't care if anyone comes to see me or not."

The Lesson

- Often a spiritual quest masks our inner need to feel important and gain community status. Many times this true motivation is hidden from the spiritual traveler.

- Grasshopper is bored and tries to use spiritual learning to change his life situation. In a sense, he is an imposter, cares little if he takes advantage of others and is brazen about it to Turtle. Being famous will provide some of the stimulation and excitement that Grasshopper is seeking.

- In a spiritual search, the traveler and teacher must be aligned through what is termed "sincerity." Both must have an inner burning for Truth.

28. THE GUIDE KNOWS

Turtle was walking down the road, when he saw Grasshopper approaching.

Turtle called out, "Friend, I am lost. Can you give me some directions?"

"Sure Turtle, where are you going?"

"I don't know."

"How can I give you directions if you don't know where you are going?"

"Well, I guess you're not the one who can help me. I'll have to keep looking for someone who knows where I am going and can point the way."

The Lesson

- Turtle is playing the part of the sincere seeker who is looking for a Guide to tell him what to do and how to do it.

- In some spiritual schools, this attitude of following direction is called submitting to the Master. This submission is an active condition, because the seeker/traveler willingly accepts this role and loves Truth. It is the Teacher, who can show this inner Truth to the student.

29. SENSORY STIMULATION

Grasshopper was sitting in the meadow pricking his leg with a thorn. Just then, Turtle happened by and couldn't believe what he was seeing.

"Dear friend, what are you doing? Surely that must hurt? A Grasshopper's flesh was not made to endure such punishment."

"Foolish Turtle, don't you know, this pricking makes me feel alive. Whenever I am bored, I just pick-up a thorn and start pricking. It makes me aware of so many sensations. You should try it sometime."

The Lesson

- Some times to find physical and emotional stimulation, some people engage in destructive behavior. Consider the activity of over-eating, drinking alcohol to excess and the use of recreational drugs. These activities, while providing some fun and excitement, when engaged in to excess, are destructive to healthy living and create problems.

- In daily life all of us require a certain amount of attention from others and a certain degree of physical and mental challenge. This is the way we are hardwired.

- However when will we learn to fill our hours with purposeful and healthy activity? Staying away from those stimulants which result in personal harm.

30. OBSESSION

Turtle was positioned by his favorite rock. He had been catching and eating silver minnows for hours. After a time, a crowd gathered. Some of the other turtles were growing worried. Finally someone found Grasshopper and brought him to reason with Turtle.

Grasshopper hopped out to the rock and inquired, "What are you doing? Don't you know you will get sick if you keep eating all those minnows?"

Turtle didn't even look up or acknowledge Grasshopper. Turtle just kept catching and eating silver minnows. After a few minutes of trying to talk Turtle out of this strange behavior, Grasshopper realized talk was useless. It was time for action. So Grasshopper picked up a nearby stick and started hitting Turtle over the head.

Finally the repeated blows caused Turtle to grow very angry and lash out at Grasshopper. "What are you doing? Why are you hitting me on the head?"

As Grasshopper jumped to safety he replied, "Your gluttony was killing you. The only way to break the spell was to divert your attention by inflicting a greater stimulus. Perhaps you better examine your behavior. One silver minnow is healthy, but 100 are deadly."

The Lesson

- Turtle is playing the part of fool once again to make a point. He is showing young turtles there is such a thing as gluttony which extends to spiritual learning as well.

- Turtle's gluttony for silver minnows or spiritual experience can result in sickness and he must be snapped out of this spell (thought process) through a jolt on the head (spiritual insight).

31. CHARITY

Grasshopper came limping up to Turtle. "Help me! Help me! I have just been robbed. They have stolen everything. Now I have nothing to live on. Turtle can you help me!"

Turtle replied, "Haven't you stored anything for an emergency like this?"

"No. I haven't. I have been living day to day. Please I am desperate and need help!"

Turtle paused for a moment and offered, "I'm sorry, but I can't help you. You are just going to have to work harder and get something extra for yourself." Then Turtle walked away.

The Lesson

- Each of us is responsible for our own lives. Part of being a responsible citizen is standing on our own two feet; even in difficult times. Through adversity we learn many lessons.

- Turtle seemingly is unsympathetic to Grasshopper's problem when Turtle doesn't offer help. Turtle is trying to teach Grasshopper, self-reliance.

32. THE EXPLANATION

Later that day young turtle caught up with Turtle. "What happened between you and Grasshopper? He is telling everyone that you are uncharitable and refused to help him. I can't believe you would do that?"

"It is true. I refused."

"Why? Why would you refuse someone who is like a brother to you?"

"The answer is simple for those who look at what came before. Over the years Grasshopper has relied upon others to solve his problems. It was time that he took some responsibility. How is it charitable to encourage Grasshopper to always rely upon others?"

The Lesson

- Sometimes we become too dependent upon others and to continue helping fosters dependence and a fear to do for ourselves.

- Turtle is trying to teach young turtle; sometimes the best way to help is not to help at all.

II - Turtle Stories

33. A QUIET MOMENT

Turtle was walking around the pond complaining to everyone about how busy he was. He had to teach silver minnow catching to young turtles. He had to go visit his mother. Winter was approaching and there were preparations to make in his burrow; he had to add more straw for warmth. Lastly he promised to visit his sister on the far side of the pond. Turtle continued on in this fashion for hours, listing the things he had to do and was growing increasingly tense.

Finally Turtle sat down exhausted from all his worrying and sighed. And as he rested beneath the willow tree, a gentle breeze began to stir the leaves. Then Turtle looked up into the sky and watched the sun setting in the west. Next he noticed a dragonfly land on a lily pad and as he watched the fly move its wings; slowly Turtle began to feel at peace.

And as he sat taking in the beauty all around him, Turtle began to realize that everything, including his problems, would be alright. In the morning there would be time for all the things he had to do, but right now it was more important to remember where he came from and where he was going. Also it was most important to enjoy the moment, because he was not promised another.

The Lesson

- In stillness, we can learn many lessons. By turning inward, it can be a time when we restore balance to our everyday lives.

- Turtle offsets his worry and anxiety by listening to another part of his awareness. This is the part that knows and helps integrate the various parts of our personality.

- Often this channel of awareness is accessed by sitting still, resting, observing, focusing inward and becoming One with Nature.

34. JUST A DREAM

Turtle was swimming around the pond, feeling the warmth of the summer sun on his shell. His first class had finished and he was waiting for the next one.

Whenever Turtle got bored of teaching silver minnow catching he would swim off and think. "Yes. He really should do something else and move on. All these years of teaching the same repetitive lessons; surely he was made for something besides minnow catching?"

Just then Turtle got a cramp in his mid-section and couldn't swim. Turtle grimaced in pain and began to sink beneath the water. And as Turtle sank to the pond bottom, he was afraid. He could hold his breath for only so long and he wasn't ready to die. If the Great Turtle would allow him to live, he wouldn't complain and happily teach minnow catching for the rest of his days. Oh, he longed to have everything the way it was.

Brring! Brring! Turtle sat up startled and reached to shut off his alarm clock. It was time to go to work. It had all been a dream! As Turtle sat eating breakfast, he began to think about teaching minnow catching.

The Lesson

- Many times our dreams offer a window into another dimension, illustrating our deepest thoughts. Also they can present symbolically what we want.

- In his dream, Turtle is confronted with the inner reality that he wants something more than teaching silver minnow catching.

- For the spiritual traveler, our sleeping hours (with our dreams) constitute a classroom. It has been suggested that the majority of the Teaching takes place at night while we are sleeping.

35. MISSED OPPORTUNITY

Turtle was crouched, hidden, behind his favorite rock waiting for breakfast to swim by. After a time, a tiny silver minnow came along, but Turtle exclaimed, 'This fellow is too small for me to waste my time on. I'll just be patient and wait until something bigger comes along."

About midmorning along came a tadpole. Turtle thought, "I like tadpoles, but I love frogs even more. I'll wait until this tadpole grows up. Then I'll really enjoy myself."

Later in the morning, Turtle was growing weak from hunger and vowed, "No matter what, I'm going to take a bite out of the next thing to swim by and have my breakfast." About 20 minutes later along came a water bug. Turtle exclaimed, "Ugh! A water bug; I hate water bugs! They're so hard." Before Turtle could change his mind, the bug was gone.

Turtle looked up at the sun and saw it was almost noon. Then Turtle remembered he was on a diet and never ate lunch. So, still hungry, Turtle began swimming back to his burrow.

The Lesson

- Sometimes it is not a matter of what we do, but that we do something. Taking action often sets in motion a chain of events and we gain the prize.

- Also procrastination makes us uneasy, nervous and fearful. To reach fulfillment, we must learn to play the different stations in our mind and know when to take action.

36. SEARCH

It was dark and Turtle was looking about his burrow muttering to himself. "Where have I put it? If I don't find it, what will become of me? Surely I am ruined!"

Then Turtle thought to himself, "Get a hold on your emotions. If you're going to be successful, you must search in an organized pattern." So Turtle devised a plan and then put it into action. First he felt around on the ceiling. Then he groped around on the floor; all without success.

After a time Turtle began to grow sad. He was afraid it was gone forever and he would never find it. Suddenly an idea occurred to him. "Perhaps I am going about this in the wrong way? What I need is a candle to help me see in the dark."

So Turtle set about the task of finding a candle and matches. This took a good part of the evening; eventually he was successful. After Turtle lit the candle and could see more clearly, he figured out his next step.

"What I will do is search the left, then the right side of my burrow." And after some hours of searching the left, without success, it was time to search the right side. But the candle was burning low and Turtle was tired. So Turtle sat down on the right side of the burrow and closed his eyes.

As the candle burned out, Turtle fell asleep. When he awoke, it was morning and lo and behold! He found himself resting beside his small bag of gold. It was undisturbed in the hole he had dug to protect it. Turtle had forgotten where it was waiting for him the whole time.

The Lesson

- While trying to solve a problem, often different factors and approaches must come together. Turtle quickly realizes that a random search isn't helping him much; so he adds a piece of technology (candle) to brighten the darkness.

- Next he devises a rationale plan and puts it to work; unfortunately, before he can complete the plan, he grows tired and falls asleep.

- As the situation develops, and as luck or fate would have it, simultaneously another part of Turtle's brain is functioning; and on a subconscious level, Turtle intuitively falls asleep right next to his gold.

- Similarly if a spiritual quest is to be successful, the right elements must combine. It must be the right time, in the right place and with the right people. Also at work must be Baraka or Divine Light to brighten the seeker's inner darkness and help find the gold. This is represented by a candle which helps lead Turtle to the spot.

37. THE CYCLE

Turtle was seated in his burrow, reflecting on the meaning of the Path and Reality. And as he rested, slowly, his soul began to sing.

"First the turtle must seek. Then seeking gives way to learning and receiving. In time learning gives way to giving. Then the Cycle is complete.

"Remember you cannot give until you have received. And you cannot receive until you have learned to accept the Truth. This can only be taught by one who traveled a spiritual path and has attained higher knowledge.

The Truth is always there. We are the ones who shut off to this Reality. The task of the Guide is to free this secret."

The Lesson

- During his meditation, Turtle contemplates the cycle of spiritual learning. This cycle is repeated over and over, and the traveler may experience the stages in sequence, simultaneously or across different 'lifetimes' with long periods of inactivity.

- For many spiritual travelers, in order for them to freely give, first, they must receive. In this way, feelings of resentment are avoided and the giver is aligned with the recipient.

38. LARGER VIEW

It was a beautiful morning and something told Turtle to take the back road to Pond. As Turtle approached the giant sycamore, which stood on the north shore, he noticed the tree was lined with scores of cocoons. As Turtle drew closer, he saw the cocoons were breaking up and beautiful butterflies, slowly, through their struggles were emerging.

Excitedly, Turtle quickened his pace and drew within ear shot. He overheard one butterfly say to another, "This struggle to break out was the most painful thing I've ever experienced. I should have stayed inside. It was so peaceful."

A second butterfly replied, "To me the struggle was beautiful. I was so happy to know, soon, I would be free. I was singing as a broke through the shell."

Then a third added, "You two are both wrong. For me there was only the realization that I was fulfilling my destiny. We are all part of the eternal perfection of the universe. To me this was not painful or joyous. For me breaking out was natural."

And as Turtle sat behind the tree, he heard all manner of comments from the young butterflies as they emerged. Turtle also noticed some could not get free and died, exhausted by their struggle.

Later as Turtle slowly walked toward the Pond he wondered, "Essentially there was only one event, the struggle to break free of the cocoon. Yet there were many views. Perhaps these individual experiences all form the bigger picture?"

The Lesson

- This larger view or inner connection pulls together seemingly disconnected factors into a mosaic or a design.

- This inner connection and the capacity to experience a Higher Reality has been called many things. Today some call this view mysticism, Higher Knowledge, Spiritual Capacity or Intuition.

- This view doesn't replace the other views, it integrates and helps take them further. Adding another layer to help some reach higher.

39. FRIGHTENED OF SELF

Turtle was pacing up and down the floor mumbling, "Who am I? Who is the real Turtle?"

Turtle proceeded to do this for hours. Finally Turtle's pacing brought him before the mirror which stood in the far corner of his burrow. When Turtle looked up and saw his own reflection in the mirror, he turned around frightened and ran as fast as a turtle can, outside. Calling all the while, "This cannot be me! This cannot be me! Do I really look like that?"

The Lesson

- From a spiritual point of view, seeing what is actually in front of you, as opposed to what we believe or have been conditioned to see, is one of the signs of advanced learning. This learning is necessary to proceed.

- Looking in the mirror, Turtle becomes frightened when he gets a real, honest look at himself.

- For the spiritual traveler, seeing our own weaknesses, strengths and need for self- importance, the way we actually are, can be a continually sobering experience.

- Often our real motives for wanting spiritual learning are deeply hidden.

- As beings of flesh and emotion, we have many needs which are all part of the Plan; yet these very real human needs must be temporarily shed for a certain type of spiritual learning/experience to occur.

40. ALL THAT GLITTERS

Turtle was resting outside his burrow and noticed a shiny object on the distant hill. As he rushed (again, for a turtle, that is) and approached the object; it continued to glitter in the sun, like a fine piece of gold. Turtle was growing excited and began to dream how he was going to spend the money from his find.

As Turtle reached over to pick-up the object, he realized it wasn't a piece of gold at all, but the shiny back of a scorpion whose shell was acting as a reflector.

Quickly before disturbing the sleepy scorpion and getting bitten, Turtle turned around and rushed as quickly as he could back to his burrow for safety.

The Lesson

- In a spiritual search, often travelers are attracted to the flashy and shiny; seeking instruction from famous, glamorous and even exotic personages. Initially these teachers look and sound really good. They may even appear on public television, the religion channel or in a large, fancy Mosque or

Church; but after a time, depending upon the circumstances, their message and instruction may waste your time, turn around and even bite you; leaving you empty.

- Most often the real hidden guides of humanity look like everyone else, live next door and spend a great deal of time deflecting potential students. They have real work to do, and unprepared, self- seeking students take up a lot of time.

- Turtle realizes at the last moment, he was mistaken to be motivated by greed; this shiny, dangerous object was not for him and potentially deadly (to his spiritual search).

41. THE RIGHT SPOT

Out of respect, Turtle decided to hang a picture of great grandfather turtle on the wall of his burrow. Great grandfather was revered by turtles as the father of modern silver minnow catching, and his picture had to be hung exactly in the right place.

At first Turtle placed the picture over his bed. Then changed his mind and moved it over the chair. Finally after hours of changing locations, as Turtle hammered the nail, the picture frame split and grandfather came crashing down.

Turtle looked at the broken picture on the floor and declared, "Aha! I knew if I kept trying sooner or later I would find the right spot!"

The Lesson

- Sometimes instead of continuing to work to get what we want, when we encounter resistance, we settle for an outcome. Further we may rationalize and convince ourselves this outcome was due to the hand of fate.

- Instead of working to correct the situation; fix the broken picture and figure out emotionally why he cannot decide upon a spot to hang the picture, Turtle convinces himself the picture looks great on the ground.

- In daily life, sometimes when we are emotionally clouded, we cannot make a simple decision; we convince ourselves what has happened is acceptable and the natural outcome of things.

42. HARMONY

Turtle was sitting by the Pond and watching the movement of the water against the breeze.

"Yes the Pond is a beautiful place and in harmony. We are the ones who fail to see this unity. When a dragonfly is consumed by the perch; other dragonflies see this event as horrible and unnatural. His relatives say, "This fly had so much to live for and he was just beginning to make real strides in the world of flies. Wasn't it horrible how he died?"

Ah, the correct attitude for the other flies would be one of acceptance, tempered by the desire not to be consumed by the perch. Of course the fly's relatives must grieve, yet, grief and anger must eventually give way to acceptance. Over time acceptance must be replaced by love. For love, slowly, leads to unity. And the Pond is always in harmony. We are the ones who break the chain by our actions without realizing it."

The Lesson

- No matter our opinion and personal view; the Pond is always in harmony. The forces which act upon the Pond are part of a larger eco-system and universe; these natural forces have been in play for millions of years. These forces include life and death, creation and destruction.

- Often we are the ones who fail to see this connection and balance; judging events by our limited view; many times disrupting the balance by our selfish, destructive action upon the natural environment.

43. DEEP INSIDE

Turtle was outside his burrow thinking to himself, "I wish that I could be like Grasshopper. He is so clever and always trying to help people. Grasshopper travels each week to see his spiritual teacher to increase his level of awareness. All I ever do is go down to the pond and work each day. What a boring life I lead!"

All afternoon, Turtle continued comparing his life with the lives of others. Poor Turtle, he never realized it is what we have deep inside and how we use our individual abilities that is really important. Others will always have more and some will have less; what we can control is who we are and the individual effort we make.

The Lesson

- Turtle makes one of the cardinal mistakes of daily thought. Comparing what he has or doesn't have with that of another; particularly someone who he sees as having more.

- While this comparison can be useful at times and push us further to change our circumstances, more often than not this thinking creates an emptiness or void. It is a mental trap of sorts.

- A more useful approach is to examine our own need, independent of others, and proceed based upon who we are and what we want, instead of comparing ourselves to someone else.

44. THINKING ABOUT HIMSELF

Having awakened from an orgy of grapes, Turtle declared, "What a stupid thing for me to do. Trying to set a grape eating record and making myself sick is not the way to achieve fame or fortune. Perhaps I should devise another plan? Let me see... we already have a famous track star and beauty queen in our family. Another is a renowned mathematician. Perhaps I can persuade Grasshopper into letting me meet his spiritual teacher? Then I can become the best student, become a saint..."

Well into the afternoon, Turtle continued in this fashion, examining a variety of grand plans. Meanwhile Turtle's mother wondered why he missed their weekly lunch, dust was mounting in Turtle's burrow and young turtles were waiting for their silver minnow catching class. Turtle had forgotten his responsibilities; being too busy for all these things.

The Lesson

- Turtle's personal thoughts and lack of action, concerning his daily responsibilities, clearly affect him and others in his life.

- Additionally, this repeating pattern about becoming famous leaves an inner impression, which at some point must be overcome. He cannot continue with this pattern and omit his responsibilities, without some very real Pond consequences.

III - Silver Minnow Catching Stories

45. SHOCKED INTO REALITY

Turtle was swimming in ever widening underwater circles. He did this on a regular basis. It was almost a compulsion with him. As his circles grew larger, he swam faster and faster. Sometimes he would go on like this for hours, finding it very difficult to stop.

So on this day, as he swam faster and faster, he didn't notice the large tree branch which had fallen into the pond. Suddenly the arc of one of Turtle's circles caused him to hit his head on the branch, rendering him unconscious.

When Turtle awoke he found himself surrounded by his students and the turtle physician. As Turtle's eyes opened, the physician declared, "I guess it will be a long time before you are able to do that again. You have to stay in bed for three weeks."

The Lesson

- Often in life we are caught in cycles, habits and repeating events unaware that we are the cause. Turtle plays the part of most creatures that are unaware they are the cause of their own problems; Turtle was not paying attention to where he was going and this resulted in injury.

- Unfortunately, it often takes a shock or failing of health to free us from these repeating habits/patterns. And in the process there is usually a price to pay.

46. PATTERNS

As Turtle lay in bed, recovering from his accident, he grew more worried. He wondered who would take care of his students. Also who was going to speak at the turtle conference next week on silver minnow catching in his place? And as Turtle thought about his obligations and his inability to fulfill them, he grew more anxious. This caused his head to ache, thereby, delaying his recovery.

If Turtle had only looked past the short term effect of his accident, he might have noticed that some of his students used their free time for independent minnow study. While others took the time to pursue other activities they were more interested in. And the fellow, who replaced him at the turtle conference, while not as skilled, gained confidence from the presentation.

Most of all Turtle might have best used the time to wonder what caused him to go around in circles; thereby helping to free him from his obsessive patterns in everyday life.

The Lesson

- Many times it is an illness or accident that teaches us the world will go on just fine without us. While we might be missed, things have a way of sorting out and adjustments are made.

- While Turtle is busy worrying about his obligations, as the story suggests, he could be using the time to figure out why he had to swim in ever widening circles.

- Turtle needed to ask, what was bothering him deep inside, causing anxiety. Often fear is at the heart of repetitive behavior. What is Turtle afraid of?

47. ALL THE FACTS

Grasshopper had come to tell Turtle that many of his students were deserting. They had grown tired of waiting for Turtle to recover and were angry that he could have been so careless in the water. Wasn't it a cardinal principle that each turtle was to survey his swimming area before engaging in extensive underwater movement? They wondered what kind of teacher could forget this beginning principle.

Before Grasshopper could bring-up the subject, Turtle began to speak. It seemed as if he again read Grasshopper's mind. "Isn't it peculiar how quick some turtles are to judge without all the facts. The branch fell into the pond after I was already in the water. I could not have anticipated that. Yet the really perceptive students will see this and realize my accident in no way affects my ability to teach them.

This accident occurred through a series of events and a weakness in me. I should have been more vigilant and watched where I was going. All my students have to be concerned about is my ability to teach them. This was not affected."

The Lesson

- We have a situation where young turtles are judging without all the facts. They view Turtle's accident as carelessness which to them means he is weak, and a real teacher is not weak, he must be perfect.

- Spiritual teachers are human and have imperfections, but have everything the student needs to make the journey. Said another way, the teacher's weakness/humanness doesn't affect the student negatively. It helps the teacher better understand the student, because they have traveled through their own personal limitations.

48. STALE BREAD

Turtle was in bed eating stale bread and disliking every bite. When Grasshopper entered the burrow he asked Turtle why he was eating hard bread.

Having never tasted soft, fresh bread Turtle replied, "Grasshopper you're such a joker. There is no such thing as soft bread."

Grasshopper just shook his head in disbelief, wondering if Turtle would ever get well.

The Lesson

- For the spiritual traveler who has never tasted real spiritual experience, worn out prayers, beliefs, rituals and exercises serve as the core of spiritual learning. These are intended as a beginning and foundation upon which real spiritual experience may be added.

- For young turtles who have never become one with the movement of the silver minnow's tail (fresh bread), the brown and grey minnow suffice (stale bread), serving as a starting point.

- Grasshopper who has a spiritual teacher and presumably has experienced real spiritual caresses, cannot understand Turtle's disbelief that there is fresh, soft bread (spiritual experience); Turtle continues to play the role of a traditional believer who is at the beginning of their journey. Someone who is satisfied with 'old' prayers and rituals (stale bread); not believing there is something higher.

49. THE PROPER WAY

Turtle and Grasshopper had been discussing some of the principles of the spiritual journey, when Grasshopper posed this question, "How can you grasp that which is ungraspable?"

Without thinking Turtle replied, "Only by reaching for it in the proper way."

As Grasshopper thought about Turtle's reply, he wondered, "What was the proper way?"

Almost, as if, Turtle had been reading Grasshopper's mind, Turtle continued, "And the proper way can only be taught by one who has Attained and reached journey's end. These principles and the method are revealed, gradually, as the student is ready."

Later, as Grasshopper hopped home he thought, "That Turtle thinks he is so smart. Who does he think he is telling me what to do? After all I am the one who has a spiritual teacher, not him."

And as Turtle rested in bed he couldn't remember anything that was said. He was too busy worrying about what he wasn't doing.

The Lesson

- Grasshopper is visiting Turtle who is still mending from his underwater accident. In their discussion, Grasshopper poses questions about the spiritual journey.

- Without thinking, Turtle answers Grasshopper's questions. After his accident and blow to the head, another part of Turtle's consciousness is operating. This is the part that knows all and is usually hidden beneath our daily cares.

- Because Grasshopper considers himself a good spiritual student with a teacher, he is put off by Turtle's correct answers; Grasshopper is unaware that he is jealous of Turtle's new ability.

- And because Turtle has not fully come back mentally, he cannot remember his responses.

50. HOLLOW WORDS

One of the younger turtles in silver minnow catching class came to visit Turtle. She was upset about his accident and wondered what would become of her and the others if Turtle didn't get well.

"Mr. Turtle what will become of us if we don't have you for a teacher? How will we learn how to catch minnows and thereby care for our family when we are older?"

Turtle thought for a moment, trying to find the right words, and replied, "Do not worry. If I can no longer perform my duties another will take my place. Remember, each of you has the inner capacity to learn and succeed. This is inborn. All I have done is helped you realize it through a variety of exercises and experiences. Many of you have already been taught the essential elements."

Not really understanding or fully comforted by Turtle's words, the young turtle thanked her teacher and left. Then Turtle lay back and thought, "If I could just believe those words myself, everything would be just fine."

The Lesson

- Turtle's accident has affected many and he himself is still struggling with this event and its outcome.

- This young turtle is worried that without her teacher she will not learn the things she needs to know to care for her future family. Turtle tries to reassure her with the very real facts of the situation, silver minnow catching is natural and if he is not there another will take his place.

- While these are the conditions of minnow catching and spiritual learning; because he has not fully recovered, part of Turtle is worried and not sure he believes events will naturally work out.

51. ONE IN A HUNDRED

Turtle recovered and was standing before his class. The number of students dropped to five. While Turtle was grateful these students remained, he realized it was important to test them further. So instead of starting the lesson, Turtle just stood in front of the group, appearing distracted.

When some of the students tried to get Turtle's attention, he pretended not to hear them. After 20 minutes of this, four students left, grumbling to each other that Turtle had lost his mind.

Finally the remaining student came forward and inquired if Turtle was feeling sick and offered to help him home. As they walked to Turtle's burrow, Turtle remembered, "Barely one in a 100 is capable of serious learning. The others may think they are learning, but few perceive the real Truth. Perhaps this young turtle has the capacity to learn?"

The Lesson

- In spiritual learning, often the Teacher plays different roles; sometimes the role of fool is used to test which students can see past superficialities and discern what is actually going on. This ability is called, "Seeing what is in front of you," not what you have been taught, through indoctrination, is taking place. Before serious learning, often a test of sorts is given.

- A student that is capable of seeing what is in front of him/her is very rare; this capacity is said to be a good indicator of one who can learn the truth.

52. ENOUGH IN IT

Two turtles were down by the pond practicing silver minnow catching. The first turtle asked the second: "Are you going to rejoin Turtle's class? You know only young turtle is attending. All the others have left."

The second replied, "I really can't make up my mind. I thought he was a good teacher but he really does some strange things. I'm not sure I can get anything out of his classes. Sometimes his behavior rubs me in the wrong way."

"Like-wise. I remember the time he told me not to go to the pond for one whole week. He wanted me to sit in my burrow and catch silver minnows with my mind. I sure caught a lot of fish that week, unfortunately none made it to my stomach."

"Yah. Think of all the criticism we are going to get from the others. Besides there are other teachers and considering all the options, I'm not sure there is enough in it for me to go back."

The Lesson

- In spiritual studies, there are many teachers and many ways of reaching the goal. These differences in presentation exist because turtles are different and what works for one may not necessarily work for another.

- While young turtles are free to pick and choose their teacher; they must be ever mindful that they can lose precious time working with the wrong teacher and path.

- It is said, that for turtles and spiritual travelers, like calls to like; and the Truth will always call to a truthful seeker.

53. WHICH DO YOU WANT TO BE?

"Silver minnow catching has always been and will continue to exist. It is the underlying force in the turtle world. Without it our society would crumble. Few really know the importance of this science. Consider where our society would be without its daily nourishment. How would we sustain ourselves and how would young turtles reach for excellence?

Silver minnow catching is more than a method to fill the turtle's belly. It is a way whereby turtles can reach their inner potential. Some young turtles are content merely to learn the basics and settle for any minnow to quiet their spiritual hunger. Others seek the perfect minnow and will go days without eating. Then there are those who are masters of the situation, and know when to eat and when to rest. They also know when to share their food. Which do you want to be?"

The Lesson

- All societies have an inner path of spiritual learning; it is the same for turtles. This inner learning of spiritual experience is in addition to other forms of learning. Spirit does not replace taking care of family and contributing positively to the world; it is additional and helps integrate other learning.

- For those students, and turtles as well, this form of learning completes the turtle. Helping them be as concerned for their neighbor as they are for themselves. True spiritual learning is the missing ingredient and helps all creatures of pond live harmoniously together, getting past their individual differences.

- Those turtles that have joined their consciousness with silver minnows; taste something finer and know all are One in spirit and part of the larger world, the Pond.

54. FIX ON THE GOAL

Turtle was down by the pond instructing young turtles in silver minnow catching. "Now the most important thing is to fix your attention on the minnow you want. Do not get distracted by the others who are swimming in the school. Keep your eyes and concentration focused on your goal; at the right moment, jump."

Just as Turtle walked down to the water to demonstrate his technique, a beautiful, young girl turtle came walking by. All eyes turned to watch her graceful movements and everyone including Turtle was distracted from the lesson.

However one young turtle remembered Turtle's words and kept focused on the minnows that were drawing near. And at precisely the right moment, the young turtle jumped and captured the prize.

The Lesson

- Some pulls in life are stronger than others. For many young turtles, it is easy to get distracted by a beautiful or handsome young turtle.

- However only the turtle who fixes on the goal captures the prize.

- Just about everyone has lapses in attention; what we need to learn is how to redirect our thoughts as they wander. One of the things silver minnow catching class does is teach young turtles how to concentrate by focusing on the movement of the minnow's tail. And as the mind wanders, turtles must be flexible enough, without getting down on themselves, and simply redirect back to the goal, movement of the minnow's tail. For most this exercise must be practiced over and over; until focusing on the goal, and when concentration fails, redirecting back, becomes second nature.

55. WHAT'S A TURTLE FOR?

All of the young turtles were down by the Pond, taking a lunch break from silver minnow catching class and catching mayflies. According to Turtle's calculations, only a few flies would make it to the afternoon.

Just then along came a flock of blue jays and they too began to feast upon the flies. This went on for a while and as Turtle sat watching the struggle that was taking place, he began to contemplate his own passing.

"Yes, the Great Turtle gives life and also takes it. What is the purpose of all the hours between? One day we are here and the next we are gone. To what purpose is all this energy and struggle?"

And as Turtle sat meditating upon these grand thoughts, one of the youngest turtles who was having trouble catching mayflies, sought him out. "Mr. Turtle, please help me. I am not as quick as the others and I am having trouble catching flies. Please show me how."

For an instant, Turtle was annoyed at being interrupted from thinking his grand thoughts, then, he smiled and said, "Sure, I'll show you. What's an older turtle for?"

The Lesson

- In every thought and action we are all creators of reality.

- Turtle, while enjoying his own thoughts, decides to put aside his meditation and help another. Positive thoughts are one form of energy and positive actions, another higher form.

- Often it is our own desires, thoughts and actions, such as meditation or prayer is always the higher form that must be pushed aside, temporarily, so we can move forward and contribute to the situation.

56. FOLLOWING THE PATH

Turtle was talking to Grasshopper about young turtles in his silver minnow catching class.

"You know when turtles are young they are easy to teach. They follow instruction and naturally learn what must be done. It isn't until they become older that the difficulty sets in. With age, turtles develop more of their personality and begin to choose whether to follow my instruction or not.

Instead of following the clearly defined path, some reject and others wish to add or change it. If they would only follow what has been laid out for them, there would be no difficulty and each would realize their inner potential."

The Lesson

- Often spiritual teaching is presented at an early age. Sometimes it is rejected and other times accepted. Yet this early learning is essential and can serve as a foundation and a beginning. Formal religion is intended as a starting point. Over time, the vibrant or living element needs to be added. However many get discouraged and never get to this point.

- Unfortunately, many spiritual teachings are shells of their former self; having decayed and lost their inner content. This fossilization causes many to turn from religion, not realizing that spiritual paths are always being updated by living teachers.

- Fortunately for young turtles in Pond, real spiritual experience is available and offered in silver minnow catching.

57. WELL, WHICH IS IT?

Turtle was getting ready to go to sleep and looking forward to his morning lesson with the young turtles. How he enjoyed teaching and helping young turtles master the skill of silver minnow catching. It was such exciting work.

In the morning when Turtle awoke he was tired. He just didn't feel like going to the pond and leading minnow catching class. Besides, he thought, "This work is so boring."

Later in the afternoon, after completing the lesson, Turtle evaluated the day's work. While some of the young turtles seemed to get it, as usual some of them didn't. On the whole, it was just an average day.

The Lesson

- Turtle confronts a range of changing emotions about work. One moment he is content, the next anxious and bored. "So which is it," Turtle asks himself.

- It is all of these feelings and more. Each person is a landscape of changing emotions and as we mature, we realize this is the way of life. Ups and downs comprising the mosaic of our changing feelings.

58. WHY TRY?

Turtle had given three young turtles an assignment to capture as many minnows as they could in a two hour period. The winner was to be awarded a silver minnow catching badge of excellence.

Before starting on their assignment, two of the turtles got into a discussion about how Turtle favored the third student. These two spent most of the period discussing Turtle's erratic behavior at times and partiality toward the third student.

Finally when it became time to tally-up, of course the third student won. She had been the only one to take the assignment seriously.

Later in the afternoon as the two turtles walked home they conferred, "See? What was the point of the exercise? We knew Turtle would give her the badge anyway."

The Lesson

- Sometimes because of preconceived ideas of what we believe, we affect the outcome of events and do not focus our energy properly.

- While these two turtles were busy complaining about Turtle, the third student was busy catching minnows. This additional time on the task pushed her over the top and she won.

- And because she won, this convinced the other two that they had been right all along. This is called a self-fulfilling prophecy.

59. WHAT THE TEACHER KNOWS

One of the younger turtles was questioning Turtle's ability to lead the class. "How do we know what you are teaching will help us learn to catch silver minnows?"

Turtle replied, "Because silver minnow catching is a perfected science. The turtles in our family have been keepers of this tradition for generations."

"Come on now. Surely you couldn't know everything there is to know about catching minnows. One turtle couldn't possibly know everything."

"I know everything the young turtle needs to know. I have caught silver minnows myself. Besides I have access to the ancient knowledge which great grandfather turtle recorded. If you believe you can find a better way to learn minnow catching, then, go ahead and learn it. If you want to learn this method, then be still and follow my instruction."

The Lesson

- One of the criteria for a teacher of the Path is that they have everything the student requires.

- Initially we have to take this on faith. When we are in the presence of a teacher, if we are learning and thinking more about the Light, this is a sign of progress and indicator of one who knows the Way Home.

- This criterion to assess a teacher works for young turtles as well. If they are learning and thinking more about minnows, they are with a true teacher.

60. WRONG TIME, WRONG PLACE, WRONG TURTLES

Turtle was standing before the class of young turtles and thinking, "I am so tired of the same old lesson. Today I will break new ground and educate these turtles as to the difference between illusion and reality. This lesson will make me famous and I will be remembered by all turtles."

So Turtle began a discourse which went something like this. "You see, everything before you, the earth, water and trees must pass. Even you will one day change into something else. All that is real is that which is lasting and can be of use in the next place. Close your eyes to the physical and emotional reality and one day, as the Great Turtle Wills, you will know Divine Truth."

By the time Turtle finished, all the young turtles had left, except one. This fellow had fallen asleep. Turtle was so wrapped up in his own words, he hadn't even noticed.

The Lesson

- In order for a teaching situation to work, certain factors must be aligned.

- Here we see how a teaching may be presented and not work, because it is the wrong time, wrong place and with the wrong turtles.

61. RIGHT TIME, RIGHT PLACE, RIGHT TURTLES

Later in the day, the young turtle that had fallen asleep came to see Turtle in his burrow.

"Mr. Turtle I am sorry that I fell asleep today in class. I started listening to your words and they filled me with so much hope and joy, but I was exhausted from yesterday's lesson and could not keep my eyes open. Can you tell me more about Divine Truth?"

Turtle had been hurt by this student's indifference, but decided to give this fellow a second chance. Hesitantly Turtle proceeded. "There is an underlying Reality which unifies all things in the universe. To some, this Reality is called Divine Truth. It is the very fabric upon which everything stands and draws their life energy. It is the mother/father of us all.

It is like mother earth who gives life to trees, grasses, fish and all manner of things. Some look at the land and see only that which is above the ground and perceive the trees or bushes as their Truth. When it is the earth from which all things draw sustenance. For the earth connects all things, as they draw their life from its fabric."

The Lesson

- As a follow up to where a teaching was presented and ignored, in this piece, we see how events come together and everything worked.

- Sometimes, a period of time must elapse and participants (Turtle) must change their view of events (young turtle's indifference). Gaining additional information, Turtle is more accepting and a teaching situation occurs.

62. WHAT DID YOU DO ABOUT IT?

Excitedly Grasshopper came hopping up to Turtle. "A crowd of young turtles are down by the Pond and making fun of young turtle. Publicly young turtle is trying to capture silver minnows with his mind."

Turtle inquired, "Well, what did you do to stop them?"

"I told them to stop making fun of things they couldn't understand."

"Did that work?"

"No, they just kept at it."

"Well, I guess it's time to do something, instead, of just talking about it."

With these words, Turtle rushed for a turtle, that is, down to the Pond and sat beside young turtle. All the while others kept making fun of young turtle. In fact when Turtle arrived the insults increased.

When Turtle focused his inner gaze upon a stream of silver minnows that were swimming by; one by one, the minnows began to jump out of the Pond and land at his feet. When the entire school was flopping about on the shore, Turtle yelled out to the crowd of young turtles, "Don't make fun of things you cannot understand."

At this sight, the crowd of young turtles quickly swam away, yelling, "Witchcraft! Witchcraft! Turtle is a witch."

Then, master and student helped the silver minnows find their way back into the Pond.

The Lesson

- In spiritual studies, slowly the traveler learns to accept possibilities within the framework/context of a teaching system or Path. Just because a traveler does not believe or know about something, doesn't make it true or untrue. Many realities are potentials waiting for the traveler to accept and believe. At present they are Truths or possibilities, waiting, beyond his/her scope or belief system.

- Sometimes in order to travel further or resolve an impasse, we require a little help from our friends (Teacher). Also it must be the right time, right place, and right time; this lesson had many dimensions and contained something for all participants to learn.

IV - Young Turtle Stories

63. PUPILS THEY DESERVE

After Turtle sat down in his burrow, he asked young turtle to remain. Without wasting a moment Turtle inquired, "Why have you stayed with me through all my difficulties? All of your friends have left, yet you remain. Why is this?"

"I don't know. I guess it is because I hope you can teach me something. Today you are ill. Perhaps tomorrow I can learn?"

Turtle thought to himself, "Sometimes teachers do get the pupils they deserve."

The Lesson

- Young turtle exhibits two qualities necessary in the student. The first is ordinary compassion; young turtle feels sympathy for Turtle's struggling health. The second capacity is a burning desire to learn even under trying circumstances.

- In silver minnow catching, as well as spiritual studies, many qualities are necessary for success. These are two important ones; another includes "love' for the Ultimate Source, coupled with a strong need to be One with the Creative Element.

64. FILLING THE EMPTINESS

Young turtle continued, "How was the method of reaching inner knowledge devised? Why were turtles created to try and reach completion?"

"Within each turtle there is an emptiness or void that can only be filled by higher knowledge. Turtles try to fill this inner emptiness with all sorts of activity and pursuits; but the emptiness remains. Ultimately we were born so we might one day learn of silver minnow catching and thereby try to uncover its spiritual secrets. The Great Turtle gave us life so we could return more complete after experiencing life fully in the pond.

"This method of inner development has always existed. It was inborn in the first turtle and passed down through the generations. It is shared with those who have inner capacity at a certain level. The teacher exists to help awaken this capacity. In this age, the method is revealed through silver minnow catching."

The Lesson

- Turtle explains that the spiritual teaching or inner core of religious experience has always existed. Also that this perennial teaching is continually being updated in a modern form which fits the time and place.

- Within each of us there is a primal, inner emptiness or unease which pushes us forward; this friction and unease can only satisfactorily be filled by the Light and spiritual learning.

65. AN ANCIENT SCIENCE

Turtle and young turtle began the lesson. "You see silver minnow catching is an ancient science. It was perfected thousands of years ago. All the young turtle must do is follow the teacher's guidance. Through the teacher's capacity to access the ancient knowledge, the teacher knows what the young turtle needs. Also, the teacher has learned silver minnow catching by the same method and is familiar with the many problems that can arise.

"Silver minnows are very elusive and in order to catch the prize, you must concentrate all your mental effort. Some turtles think that if they learn one technique that is all they will need. Little do they realize, silver minnows come in different shapes and sizes. Also, at different times of the year, the minnow's habits change and other factors like water flow, rock shadow and noise influence a turtle's capacity to succeed.

"Yet the most important factor in silver minnow catching is the student's ability to submit to the situation. This you proved to me today by submitting your needs to mine. A successful student is able to control his own personality and become one with the minnow's consciousness. By sensing what the minnow needs, the turtle can react to the situation and master it.

This inner capacity to bend one's needs to what the situation requires must already be in the student. All the teacher can do is further awaken this capacity and help refine it. The teacher cannot give it to the student."

The Lesson

- In all things what is necessary for success is hard work, inborn ability, a good teacher and 'tajali' or Divine luck/destiny.

- Here Turtle outlines for young turtle some of the specific requirements necessary for silver minnow catching success.

- Young turtles must submit their will temporarily to the situation and become one with the minnow's mind; thereby knowing the direction the minnow will take.

- This is done through a meditation of sorts; consciously focusing on the minnow's tail movement.

66. REACHING COMPLETION

"You said silver minnow catching is an ancient science whereby turtles may reach completion. "If this is so," inquired young turtle, "Will I be one of those who reaches this goal?"

Turtle paused and looked directly into young turtle's eyes for what seemed minutes and softly replied, "Silver minnow catching is the method by which turtles may access the ancient knowledge. It is the super highway to the Great Turtle and is a microcosm of the larger universe. By submitting to this way of life, you may reach completion. This is dependent on three factors: your inner capacity, your teacher's knowledge and the Will of the Great Turtle. This is a perfected science and has been this way for 1000 years. Nothing is left to chance.

"As the Great Turtle Wills, if you follow my instruction, your needs will be met."

The Lesson

- In a spiritual quest, a number of factors are essential to success. Three of these are offered.

- Key to young turtle's eventual success is Grace and Higher Design; along with a burning love in his heart.

- Silver minnow catching is a worldly form in which spiritual learning occurs. For turtles, daily elements must combine within the formula: right time, right place and right turtles. In daily life, this learning takes place around the pond catching minnows and silver minnows.

67. STRANGE BEHAVIOR

Next young turtle inquired, "I have heard stories and seen how foolish you can act. For example that day at the pond, when the remaining students were awaiting instructions, you appeared to be staring off into space. Why did you act like that? Or the time when you called yourself the World-Famous Diver? What is the meaning of your strange behavior?"

"Sometimes I play the fool, other times the teacher. Each action is in accord with the situation and the higher law. The day at the pond, with the other students, was a test to determine who was interested in more than filling his belly. Those who wanted to learn to catch minnows for food will find a suitable instructor. Those like yourself who perceive something more in minnow catching, will strive for the inner meaning regardless of instructor.

"When I put on my mask and cape and acted like a circus performer, it was done to show the others how easily swayed we are by our need for fame and fortune. For those who look deeper, there were other meanings. The spiritual quest was symbolized by my entrance into the water.

Whereas the mask and cape indicated that in order for a turtle to be successful, he had to become a stranger to the everyday world and focus on inner dimensions.

"And as the student is able to perceive with an inner eye there is more."

The Lesson

- Turtle explains to young turtle some of his mysterious and seemingly senseless actions. He was playing the part of ordinary reality, which on the surface has one type of meaning, yet to the spiritual traveler underlying this all is another dimension.

- By playing the part of fool, Turtle is "shouting out" to others. In action teaching, reality is much more than we normally see. You must look deeper, with spiritual sight, for the connecting meanings.

68. THE SAME METHOD

Turtle said to young turtle, "You see many are the teachers who try to mold the student to a particular format. Rare is the teacher who adapts the format to fit the student.

"While I am teaching silver minnow catching and the goal for everyone is to achieve consistent success, my methods must adapt to different students. Some turtles are afraid to jump into the water and others are eager. Are the two alike? Of course not! Then how can they be taught in the same way.

"Beware of the teacher who forces everyone to follow one prescription."

The Lesson

- Flexibility is an essential element in teaching, spiritual studies and silver minnow catching.

- While uniformity may be essential in early stages, all advanced learning has the capacity to adapt to the learner's unique characteristics.

69. HAPPINESS

Young turtle complained, "I am so unhappy. I don't know what to do. I thought by taking silver minnow lessons I would be fulfilled. But I am so unhappy. I just don't know what to do."

Without looking up from the pond, intent upon catching a silver minnow, Turtle whispered. "Existence is much more than happiness. It is sorrow, joy, pain, happiness, love and anger. It is all these things and more. For beyond the pond you see there is another world, and here we can experience the underlying Unity. If you are looking just for happiness, you are missing the point of this life."

And at precisely the right moment, Turtle lunged forward and captured the prize. Then he offered the silver minnow to young turtle.

The Lesson

- Many times turtles go on a spiritual quest to find happiness. Turtle points out to young turtle that spiritual learning is in addition to all the other parts of life.

- From Turtle's perspective, happiness is transitory and one emotion among many.

The World of Pond Stories

- Further, Turtle shows young turtle one way to find happiness; helping another and offers young turtle a silver minnow.

70. REACHING A MINNOW'S MIND

Young turtle was pondering Turtle's words and could not fully understand them.

"Silver minnow catching is as natural as breathing. In this process, the turtle must join his consciousness with that of the minnow thereby knowing in what direction the minnow will swim.

"The ability to subdue one's ego and thereby pick-up the minnow's thoughts and impulses can be refined. The capacity to do this is inborn and the teacher points this out to the student. Under the teacher's direction, the student enhances this ability and is able to reach the goal. Some advance quickly and others take longer."

Young turtle just shook his head. "What kind of nonsense is this about reaching a minnow's mind? I didn't even know they had one."

The Lesson

- Young turtle is struggling with the notion of quieting his everyday mind and switching his consciousness to that part which is ordinarily still.

- That is the part which is spiritual and generally operates only when the everyday thoughts are quiet. It is said, "That we submit/quiet our ego so another part will come forward. This is our spiritual awareness which is able to join with the consciousness/mind of the minnow."

- This shifting of consciousness works much like switching stations on a radio or television set.

71. THE ORGANIZATION

Young turtle inquired, "Is this the only pond where silver minnow catching is taught by the ancient methods?"

Turtle replied, "In every pond across the land where there are turtles and silver minnows, as required, the lessons are taught. Conditions may be such that the method is not required in a given pond at a particular time. However, as conditions change and the teachings are needed, student and teacher meet.

"You see nothing is left to chance. There is an organization of turtles that monitor conditions and influence factors. They oversee and make certain that silver minnow catching is in balance with the evolution of the turtle world. Silver minnow catching is the underlying energy basis of our society. It is the spiritual and material heart of our existence and is adapted to time and place."

Young turtle asked, "Do you mean there are turtles that watch over us and influence our decisions and lives?"

"That is exactly what I mean. Do not worry. This is the way it has always been and no action is taken that is not in harmony with the evolution of the turtle world and the greater good."

The Lesson

- Turtle explains to young turtle that silver minnow catching has existed since the beginning of time. It is the ancient method by which turtles access their higher consciousness. This path is available in all ponds and all times. While the external form of the teaching may vary, internally or spiritually, the path is universal and transcendent.

- This form of learning and the evolution of the turtle world are guided by a hierarchy of spiritual masters. That is the tradition.

72. YOUNG TURTLE'S ENLIGHTENMENT

Later that evening, young turtle sat down and gazed into the fire. Slowly the flames hypnotized him and he saw within the fire a panorama of his life. He saw his birth and his future death at the hand of a poisonous snake. And all the while, he was not afraid. All he felt was a quiet peacefulness and the growing realization of his own spirituality.

Within the flames, he saw silver minnows and realized for the first time that these rare, darting fish, in some strange way, symbolized the illusive nature of spiritual awareness. These minnows were always swimming about the Pond, but unless young turtle looked past the need for food, he would never unlock the mystery. For him, these silver streaks were his spiritual journey.

And as young turtle continued to sit before the flames, he was at peace. He was warm and unafraid. His Higher Self had awakened and was there to protect him against the long, cold night.

The Lesson

- By concentrating and watching the fire's flames, young turtle receives a flash of inner wisdom. He views the panorama of his life, the living and dying, realizing it is all part of the One.

- Also he sees that spiritual learning is part of his journey; helping him connect with his Higher Destiny and leading a richer life.

Dr. Stewart Bitkoff

V - Meadow Stories

73. THREE SISTERS

Once there was a dandelion that had three beautiful, yellow children. These sisters used to play in the wind together and were known across the meadow for their sweet fragrance and striking color. One morning, as the three sisters opened to the sun, the appearance of one of the flowers was changed. Its blossom, although fuller, was now comprised of tiny, white seedlings.

The two other sisters were frightened by their sister's new appearance and questioned, "What has happened to you? Are you alright?"

Gently the third sister replied, "Do not be frightened. I know I look different, but inside I am still the same. Remember mother said this was a natural process. Also, there is a voice inside me that is whispering, "You have been waiting for this all your life."

As the days passed, the two sisters grew embarrassed by their sister's altered appearance and rarely spoke to her. This made the third sister very sad, but her inner voice told her not to give-up. Eventually, she would know the meaning of her new state.

One windy afternoon as the three sisters swayed on the building breeze, the small, white seedlings detached and lifted up into the wind. And as the seedlings sailed across the meadow, searching for a place to land and make their new home, the flower rejoiced.

The next morning, there were only two sisters left to open to the sun and both had turned white.

The Lesson

- Change is the Divine chord of the universe; daily like the dandelions we grow closer to our journey upon the wind.

- Remember surrendering to the breeze is as natural as breathing; and it is only our fear that blinds us to the excitement of new life spreading across the meadow.

74. WHEN YOU ARE FLYING

A young sparrow was complaining to her mother, "You are always showing me how to fly. You have shown me all your techniques and regularly discussed the various principles involved, but when will I actually take off and fly? I am tired of practicing and preparing. When will I fly?"

In an even tone, the mother replied, "When you are ready."

"How will I know when I am ready?" continued the youngster.

"When you are flying," replied the mother.

The Lesson

- The inner awareness, once awakened, becomes an essential, conscious part of you. In the case of the young sparrow, it as natural as flying.

- The question to be asked "Is how do I awaken this capacity? What preparations do I need to make?"

- In part that is the role of the mother/teacher; to assist in this preparation.

75. EMOTIONAL REACTION

A young spider had just spun his first web and was anxiously waiting for dinner to arrive. When night came, his web was empty so he decided to go to sleep and dreamed of delicious flies for breakfast. In the morning his web was still empty and he decided to make some changes. First he doubled the size and then he decreased the space between various strands.

When nothing happened all day, he decided to ask his mother for some advice. She listened to his story then inquired as to the web's location. When she was satisfied the web was in the right place, she prescribed the following. "When the web and belly are empty, it is time to go hunting. You must capture your own meal and bring it back to the web. If you are unsuccessful, in two days return to the web and wait."

So the young spider went out and tried to capture his own fly by jumping on it. Of course he was unsuccessful and when two days passed, he returned. Lo and behold, two flies were waiting for him all tangled in his web. Quickly the spider ate the first and wrapped the second for later.

When he asked his mother how she could predict this would happen, she replied, "I have seen this many times. Your web was fine. What was lacking was patience. By prescribing something to keep your mind busy, the rest took care of itself. Next time remember the fault may not be in the circumstances but your reaction to them."

The Lesson

- One of the most difficult things for young spiders to learn is patience. Particularly when their belly is empty.

- Mother spider had seen an empty web many times. She prescribed an activity to keep her youngster busy and might even result in a snack.

- Because she had seen this situation, she realized the missing ingredient was time and patience.

- Similarly in a spiritual search what is required is the right combination of factors. That is why a guide is often essential to success.

76. THREE ANTS ON A LOG

Once there were three ants floating on a log down a fast moving stream. The first ant nervous and impatient to make his escape leaped into the water and began swimming with all his strength toward shore. Quickly he grew tired in the churning water and drowned. Weighing and considering all his options, the second ant decided to burrow into the wood, in the hope one day the log would come to rest on a distant shore. Eventually, this fellow was destined to die of starvation.

The third, an ant of perception, waited until the moment was right and leaped to a branch from a low hanging bush. As the log continued on its journey along with the second ant, the ant of perception made his escape to shore.

The Lesson

- The first two ants represent the majority of humanity, making decisions in the emotional and intellectual realm. The third ant represents our intuitive ability or higher perception.

- Each mode of consciousness is available to everyone. Consider how you make important decisions. Which realms do you operate in?

77. HAND OF FATE

Two young worms were crawling about the worm farm discussing their bright future. The first who was the larger of the two boasted, "Someday I am going to be the King of all the worms. I will win honor by defeating all you smaller worms. Then everyone will know my name and come to me for advice and help."

The second worm that was also large for his age was not as ambitious as the first, but he too had dreams of the future; and added, "Someday, I would like to be able to say I climbed every hill and traveled each tunnel in this land. I will have seen everything there is to see and everyone also will know my name."

Then the first worm replied, "Our futures look so promising. Perhaps I will even make you the official explorer to my court."

As the two worms basked joyfully in their plans for the future; the farmer's hand descended into the soil and scooped them both up.

The Lesson

- While it is good to have plans for the future and something to work toward; these plans must be aligned with your potential or design of the situation.

- In order to attain goals, everyone must have talent, hope, and plan and work hard. However, keep in mind, there may be other factors at play.

- Fate and the Unseen Forces may have something different to say about our future.

78. BE A BEETLE

A beetle was buried beneath a ton of earth and began to scream, "Help me! Help me! I am buried alive! Surely I am going to die!"

After sobbing for hours, suddenly the beetle realized he wasn't dead. Then it occurred to him he was a beetle and beetles were supposed to be in the ground.

Later, after further thought, he began climbing through the earth, toward the daylight and other adventures.

The Lesson

- For the spiritual traveler, there is a period of inner search and turmoil.

- Then one day, we remember and realize that we are also of spirit and begin reaching upward toward our more lasting lives.

79. YOUR TEACHER'S WORDS

Two flies were circling some fly paper and discussing the relative merits and dangers of landing. The first fly warned, "You know we shouldn't land on this paper. Didn't our teacher tell us that no matter how appealing the fragrance, we should avoid the paper!"

"Yes. I know he did. But I cannot control myself. I must have a taste. Besides I have made a study of the situation and I am strong enough, should I get stuck, to work my way free of the paper. Are you going to join me or are you afraid?"

"You go ahead. I will wait for you at home."

Some days later, the second fly returned. His wings were shattered and he had to crawl home. For the rest of his days, all he could talk about were those agonizing hours he spent trying to free himself from the paper.

And the second fly helped to care for his lame brother and lived to reach the end of his journey.

The Lesson

- On a spiritual journey, the traveler must have proper guidance and the good sense to follow it.

- The two flies represent conflicting aspects of our personality. The first fly wants to do things his own way and the second fly, representing the part that knows, follows his teacher's instruction and avoids a costly mistake.

80. SNAIL'S VIEW

Two snails were having a race up a rock. The first snail said, "I'm the fastest creature who ever lived. No one has ever been faster!"

The second snail thought, as he raced up the rock, "If I can keep up with this fellow, then, I, too will be the fastest creature who ever lived."

After a very long, long, time both snails arrived at the top of the rock at precisely the same moment.

Then both snails started down the rock to tell the whole snail world of their speedy exploits.

The Lesson

- In your own mind, you might be the fastest creature (snail) alive; until along comes an ant and shows you real speed.

- No matter your personal view of reality, there is always a larger, grander view.

- The reality of a situation may be much different than you imagine.

81. SELF-IMPORTANCE

Two honeybees were flying from flower to flower gathering pollen. The first said to the second, "Hurry, hurry, we have to get to the flowers before the others. I want to be the best gatherer of pollen that I can be. I want to reach my full potential and show the Queen Mother who is best."

The second bee thought, "That is a fine goal, but I have no such desire to impress the Queen. I gather pollen because it is my job and I want to do it well. Besides I don't know what else to do."

So after a time, when their sacks were full the two bees returned to the hive. And as the Guard to the Hive examined each sack, only the second bee's load was accepted.

The Lesson

- Many times it isn't always a question of what we do, but why we do it. Often personal motives are essential to how an under taking is perceived and accepted by others.

- Consider a gift given out of love, although less costly, many times is worth more to the recipient than a more costly item given only to impress.

82. ROTTEN LUCK

A fly was buzzing around the head of a cow. Finally it landed on the cow's ear. Quickly the cow twitched and frightened the fly away.

Later the fly returned and having learned its lesson landed on the cow's hind leg. As the fly took a bite, the cow swatted the fly with its tail.

As the fly fell to the ground he exclaimed, "I've always had rotten luck. I'm being punished for my past sins!"

The Lesson

- Karma or the Law of Cause and Effect can be seen daily in life.

- Here the fly is bothering the cow who simply swats the fly with its tail. Not heeding an earlier warning, when the cow twitched its ear, the fly blames his fate/luck on past sins.

- This is simply the Law of Cause and Effect working.

83. WAITING DEEP WITHIN

An acorn fell from an oak tree and lay frightened on the meadow floor. As he lay in this new environment, he remembered his past life, high on the branches. Many of his friends were still there and he longed for the companionship, the grand view of things and boasting together about their future.

As time wore on, other acorns were lost to squirrels, some failed to mature and many fell to the earth. These were hidden to each other by the fallen leaves and meadow grass.

Lying on the meadow floor for weeks, our acorn thought all was lost. Finally for safety he decided to burrow into the ground and grow some roots for stability, just inches below the earthen floor. When winter brought its blanket of snow, for many long days, the acorn felt like he would freeze to death. He wished he had never left the branches.

In time when the sun grew stronger, and the snow began to melt, the acorn felt strange stirrings. These inner movements were strong and painful; the acorn wondered if he would break apart?

When spring arrived, the acorn was no more. Instead, a smiling young sprout had taken its place and was reaching upward in glorious splendor; striving to take its place in the morning spring sunlight.

Forgotten was the hour of struggle.

The Lesson

- Each traveler is a potential waiting to bud. Each has a capacity planted deep within; yearning to reach up and caress the Light.

- Our job is to let this process unfold and in the right balance provide the necessary nutrients.

84. A SECOND CHANCE

Two snowflakes were discussing what the future held. The first snow flake said, "When I land on the ground, I am going to be part of the season's first snow. Some young child will use me to make her first snowball."

The second flake didn't know what she wanted and just listened. As the wind brought them closer to the ground the first flake spotted a young child and called out, "This is where I get off." This snowflake then proceeded to fall with the others.

The second flake couldn't decide what she wanted and stayed with the storm cloud, until she was forced to fall on the mountains with the remaining snowflakes. All during the winter months, as she lay on the mountain peak, she thought about what she wanted and finally decided. She wanted to be just like her friend. But how could that be? She had already fallen to the ground and would not get another chance. Or so she thought.

When the spring came, all the snowflakes melted together and slowly evaporated into the air. They were picked-up as mist by a passing cloud and there they remained until winter.

As the weather grew colder, the cloud began to change and gradually got ready for the first snow.

Although unaware of her previous decision, this time the snowflake chose to fall with the first snow and was used to build a snowman.

The Lesson

- Sometimes we are unsure what we want and by being indecisive, a choice that we later realize we wanted passes us by.

- Yet there is always another tomorrow and if fate so deems it possible, we get another chance.

- Many people believe this is also true of life times. As the sun rises to begin another day, we have multiple lifetimes, in many different realities.

85. A DIFFERENT VIEW

A young chick who was not content to play the games the others played or eat the food the others ate went on a journey. She decided to climb the hill overlooking the farm and see what she could see.

As the young chick climbed the hill she remembered her mother's warning. "Be content with what you have. Here in the barnyard you are safe and have food. Over there is danger and you will never be the same."

However, the young chick knew it was her destiny to climb the hill, and as she climbed it grew cold and dark. Resting for the night, the young chick was frightened, but when morning came she continued on.

Late in the afternoon of the next day, she reached the top of the hill. When she looked out across the valley and saw her farm as but one small piece of the valley floor with trees, roads, other farms and streams as part of the larger world, she fell away in a swoon.

Days later, when she returned to the farm to tell the others what she saw no one believed her. To this day, she lives apart from the other chickens and is only visited when there is a problem in the barnyard. Miraculously, she is able to offer advice and direction and is always correct.

The Lesson

- Inside each of us is unease and inner burning which pushes us forward. Also present is a need to express ourselves in the world and embrace our individual destiny.

- The young chick strongly experiences this inner restlessness and desire to find out who she is. Something inside is calling her to climb the nearby hill and see what lies beyond barnyard life.

- Once she experiences what is beyond her daily world, the greater valley; she is changed. This expanded view represents our spiritual awareness, and now the young chick has both sets of consciousness operating.

- This additional capacity, spiritual sight, sets her apart from others and becomes very useful in barnyard life.

86. SYLVESTER'S HISS

Sylvester the snake was very lonely and wanted friends. None of the other creatures in the meadow wanted to play with him. They were afraid of his fangs, bite, and terrible hiss. Although Sylvester rarely bit anyone and this occurred only when he needed to eat, the meadow creatures were frightened and stayed away.

One day Sylvester realized it was his fangs and terrible hiss that stood between him and having friends. So Sylvester promised himself that no matter what, he would not bite, show his fangs or hiss. Sylvester changed his diet, ate meadow grass and learned to control his terrible hiss. Over time, he even forgot how to hiss and bite.

Slowly, birds, field mice, squirrels, hedgehogs, and all meadow creatures realized Sylvester lost his hiss. Now creatures came to the meadow in large numbers. No one was afraid of the meadow snake and it was a great place to find food.

Although Sylvester no longer bit or used his terrible hiss, no one wanted to be friends with a snake. Some creatures that had lost friends to Sylvester's hiss used this opportunity to get even. Each time they came to the meadow, they threw rocks and sticks. Over time, Sylvester grew battered and bruised. Not only was he lonely, but he was growing thinner because he ate meadow grass. Sylvester was a pathetic sight.

One afternoon, as fate would have it, Sylvester's Mama came for a visit. Mama snake brought some of Sylvester's younger brothers and sisters to see how a full-grown snake operates. Mama was unaware of the recent changes that had come over Sylvester.

When Mama saw Sylvester in his tattered, shriveled, and bruised condition, she was shocked. Mama cried, "Sylvester what happened?"

Sylvester sobbed and told Mama the whole story. Mama listened closely, as Sylvester explained how he lost his hiss and how the other creatures took advantage. All this happened, Sylvester said, because he wanted friends and to be liked.

Mama replied, "Sylvester, you have to be who you are. Snakes bite, have fangs and are supposed to hiss. This protects us from others, helps us get food and is necessary for our lives."

As the days passed Sylvester worked on what Mama said. Slowly Sylvester found his hiss, and returned to a diet of meadow creatures. In time meadow life was the way it was meant to be and creatures, when they heard Sylvester's hiss, knew to stay far away.

The Lesson

- Each traveler must be true to who they are; often we get into trouble when we try to be something we are not.

- Sometimes troublesome situations cannot be managed without force. In order to protect ourselves, we must show courage and stand up for our convictions and needs.

Book II

The Turtle Prophecy

Man/woman is the philosopher's stone

And has within a precious jewel.

With the guidance of one who has Attained

A miraculous transformation can occur.

Yet that which is deeply hidden

Becomes manifest

Only after a confluence of essences.

-SB

Dr. Stewart Bitkoff

Table of Contents

List of Characters	201
Chapter 1 - Journey Begins	203
Chapter 2 - Evil Enters	209
Chapter 3 - Alfonses Berry Day	216
Chapter 4 - Nerge & Kwingdale Go On Vacation	225
Chapter 5 - The Storm Rages	232
Chapter 6 - Mud Slide	238
Chapter 7 - Spiritual Energy Boost	248
Chapter 8 - Deception Continues	256
Chapter 9 - Killing For Fun	266
Chapter 10 - Seeing The Future?	272
Chapter 11 - Water Parade	279
Interpretations	287

LIST OF CHARACTERS

Turtle: Turtle is our main character. In Pond he is teacher of silver minnow catching, and is on a mysterious spiritual journey.

Nerge & Kwingdale: Two field mice who have unfulfilled dreams and return to Berryville for the Annual Alfonses Day Festival.

The Riishi: One of the hidden guardians of the Plan that reflect the Light of Eternity into the physical world daily.

Sisters of Yor: Three dark entities who combine their strength to enable the Darkness to enter the physical world.

Wolf Cub: Young cub who has lost his mother and who the Sisters use to help launch their evil Plan.

Mice of Berryville: Berryville is an idyllic community of field mice who have been living in relative safety for hundreds of years; famous for its sweet berries and yearly festival.

Alfonses Berry: Founder of Berryville and patriarch of the field mouse community.

Darkness/It/Brown She-Wolf: After the Sisters combine their powers, and trick wolf cub into helping, the Darkness enters the physical world as a large, brown wolf.

CHAPTER 1 - JOURNEY BEGINS

A Turtle was swimming upriver against the current straining all the way. He had to exert all his energy not to be pushed back. The current was strong and finally Turtle gave up and sank to the bottom of the river. It was calm down below the surface and as Turtle realized this he began swimming upriver again.

◆

Nerge and Kwingdale were two field mice who had their burrow beneath the roots of a large oak tree. They scavenged for food like others of their kind and lived from day to day. Yet both of these mice had dreams. Nerge wanted to be a preacher and help lead mice to the Great Mouse in the sky. Often Nerge would stand beside the road and give impassioned speeches to his imaginary flock of followers. All the other creatures who lived in the field beside the oak, thought Nerge was a little eccentric, to say the least.

Kwingdale in his own way varied from the others. His secret dream was to be a king; a benevolent king respected for his generosity and wisdom. Unfortunately this inner need got distorted and

Kwingdale was all too quick to boss Nerge around. This was the only way Kwingdale could express this inner desire. However Kwingdale was extremely frustrated because Nerge seemed to have a mind of his own and rarely followed direction.

♦

High on a distant mountain the Riishi sat perceiving the subtle influences, directing the Light. This was the way it was and the way it had always been. The Riishis were the guardians of the hidden kingdom and participated in the Plan.

Turtle, Nerge and Kwingdale had all become part of the Plan. Yet they were unaware of their participation. It was the Riishi's job to make sure the Plan was fulfilled and to help guide these unsuspecting heroes.

Below the fast moving water Turtle continued swimming upriver. As he swam he wondered what pushed him forward. Why was he on this journey?

About a week ago, he felt a burning restlessness. No matter what Turtle did that day, the chores around the burrow or his daily lesson with the young turtles, he was distracted and could find no peace. When Turtle got like this, and it happened enough times in the past, he knew he had to wait for the inner command. Turtle's higher consciousness was sending a message and he had to be patient and see what form it would take.

As Turtle paced around the burrow, trying to work off some energy, he heard the inner words, "Swim upriver." It was a quiet voice but firm and Turtle knew it would be useless to try and resist. In the past when he tried to resist this made him worse; he became more tense and restless.

So five days ago Turtle set out on a journey. He left all of his responsibilities in Pond and began swimming upriver, stopping only to sleep and eat. Where this journey would end he did not know. He was committed to it by something he couldn't explain, only perceive and feel.

♦

Each morning, Nerge and Kwingdale awoke and gathered berries and nuts. After this chore they were free for the rest of the day. There was plenty for them to do. They could sit beside the road and talk with the passing travelers or go into the field and visit with friends. Usually their days did not vary much from this pattern of gathering and amusement. Sometimes Nerge and Kwingdale wondered if there wasn't more to life.

Nerge and Kwingdale had been friends for many years and decided to team up when they were teenagers. The pattern of raising a family and worrying about little mice was not for them. As others were finding mates and picking out a burrow, Nerge and Kwingdale sought another path.

One day in the forest Nerge and Kwingdale met. Nerge was giving a sermon to his imaginary flock. Kwingdale was out for a walk and stopped to listen.

"Oh children of the Great Mouse, is there not something more to life? Why are you content to search for food, raise a family and amuse yourselves? Don't you realize there is something else? Each child of the Great Mouse is born with the capacity to reach upward and make of themselves a vehicle to experience the Oneness of the Great Mouse. We were born to become more than we are..."

And as Kwingdale listened to Nerge, instantly he felt a kinship with these words; for he too had a dream, an aspiration to become something more than he was. Kwingdale always felt he could lead and help others. This was his dream, his higher purpose. Kwingdale never heard anyone speak of the Great Mouse in this way and waited for Nerge to complete his sermon. In time their bond grew and eventually they decided to team up to realize their dreams.

◆

Each was a child of the Light and perceived the Light in their own way. The Riishi knew it was important for each creature to maintain their view of the Cosmic Reality until they were able to accept a higher view. Within each creature's journey there were many opportunities to reach higher. Part of the Riishi's responsibilities was to make these opportunities available.

From time to time, opportunities were made available to entire communities; one such event was about to happen. The influences were coming together; the Riishi watched and waited until he had to direct the Light and participate in the Plan.

Always in a hidden way since the beginning, the Riishis worked to serve the Light. By reflecting the Light to various individuals the Plan had been moving forward since the beginning of time. What had been hidden was about to become manifest and none of the participants would ever be the same.

The Riishi knew that he too must move on and once the Plan was enacted, he had to change into something else. Yet he was not worried. This was the way it had been and would continue to be. Another had been selected to take his place and when the time came he would pass the robe.

◆

Deep within the forest where no sunlight ever reaches the Sisters of Yor hovered above a fallen animal. These Daughters of Darkness waited centuries to hatch their evil plan.

A wolf cub had been found who was without a mother and was nearing death. The cub must be free of sin and willingly choose the Darkness to preserve its life. This was the first step.

As the cub lay alone and afraid drawing nearer to death, the Sisters waited to present the cub with a Choice.

In another part of the forest life continued as it always had. The field mice gathered berries and nuts unaware of the forces that were about to descend upon their community. While their parents gathered food the little mice went to school and each was unaware of the cloud that was gathering near Berryville.

CHAPTER 2 - EVIL ENTERS

As the Riishi sat meditating he saw the community of field mice content with their lives. For as long as anyone could remember their lives had been free of danger and the supply of berries and nuts plentiful. They had lived this way for centuries; the culture they created was built upon certain premises which were about to be challenged. All of this was going to end and fear would enter their lives.

For those who accepted it, life in Berryville was safe and stable. Yet within this ideal community, the Riishi knew there was a missing element. The purpose of life was to identify this missing piece and become one with it. What was missing was the Light. This emptiness was created so it might be filled; each creature must participate in the Plan and at some point realize their kinship with the Light.

The community of field mice, while happy on a superficial level had stagnated internally. They had lost the ultimate purpose of existence and replaced it with a life of work, family and friends. There were celebrations and festivals. There were community meetings and charities for their fellow mice. Schools were built for the study of berries and nuts. Yet rarely were mice ever told there were other worlds beyond this one and a mouse remained incomplete unless he prepared for the next part of the journey.

Any mouse who wanted more than gathering and amusement was outcast or ignored until he left. Nerge and Kwingdale were recent examples of this.

◆

To Turtle, swimming upriver had become natural. It no longer was a strain. Everyone knows how difficult it is to swim against the current but Turtle had mastered this skill. Once he realized he could make better time below the surface, Turtle was able to keep a steady pace.

As Turtle continued swimming the doubts returned. Why did he listen to the inner voice? What did he hope to accomplish? While one part of Turtle's mind questioned, another part answered. "Be still. You know why. You did not imagine this. As you found higher knowledge through silver minnow catching so you must serve by swimming against the current. Be patient. The answers will come."

Pushing forward, Turtle turned his thoughts to silver minnows and minnow catching. For him this had been the path to higher knowledge. Through the world of silver minnows and becoming one with their consciousness, Turtle experienced his own transcendent self. By focusing upon the minnow and losing himself in the minnow's movement, Turtle's higher consciousness awoke. In those rare moments of intense concentration, the window of the mind opened and Turtle could perceive all kinds of things. In time, Turtle used this perceptive ability to be a better teacher to young turtles and answer personal questions in his own life. This additional ability to know was part of Turtle and linked in some way to the Great Turtle.

Through this personal spiritual experience, Turtle knew there was a Great Turtle who cared about him. When this part of the consciousness was operating, speculation left and knowledge entered. Turtle knew this journey had meaning and he was not deluded. In time the doubting part of the mind would be convinced.

Nerge was resting in his burrow thinking about his life. In fact he was feeling a little sorry for himself. Daily he walked along the road, found a spot and started to preach. Often no one stopped to listen but he kept talking and calling everyone to Truth. Truth to Nerge was love of the Great Mouse and calling everyone to this Reality.

Occasionally an ant or dragonfly would stop to listen; usually not for very long. Sometimes they would ask a question or two. "How can an ant worship or believe they are made from a mouse? Why would a mouse take the time to make an ant?"

Nerge had grown accustomed to this sort of question and had a ready answer. "It does not matter to Him. He made all creatures large and small. Each serves a purpose and is loved by the Creator. As you proceed along the path, in time, you too will come to believe it." Usually the listener would shake their head, not believing in an all-knowing Mouse and proceed along the path alright, but far away from Nerge.

In all the years Nerge had been doing this he couldn't recall a single convert. Once he came very close. As he recalled the incident, Nerge smiled to himself. It was late in the afternoon and shadows had begun to line the road. Nerge was energetically proclaiming the beauty of service to the Great Mouse and a young mouse sat down and started to listen. This fellow sat for nearly ten minutes with attention fixed on Nerge nodding agreement at all the proper times. Nerge felt more and more confident and was gathering momentum with each word. Finally Nerge worked up enough courage to ask, "Friend, are you ready for the oath of brotherhood to the Great Mouse?" This was the first time that Nerge had gotten this far and expectantly waited for an answer. Cautiously the stranger replied, "I don't know if I am ready for the oath but I am ready for the berry bread. There are refreshments after the service aren't there?"

Even Nerge had to laugh at this one. Well it was time for the berries. When he got like this the only remedy was to eat. Berries made him feel alive and to date his record was 47 berries without stop. So Nerge got up, went to the berry pile and started to eat.

As he swallowed he counted: 6, 7, 8, 9. Nerge wondered, "Why am I doing this? The last time, I was sick for two days." But Nerge kept right on swallowing 12, 13 and 14.

Kwingdale was out in the forest searching for grey nuts. These were his favorite and if they were picked in the last week of April they were extra sweet. In his own way, Kwingdale considered himself a grey nut expert. It was only after years of eating that he bestowed this title upon himself.

Kwingdale stood before the grey nut bush and called out, "My lovelies prepare for your end. You are about to be consumed by the Lord of grey nuts, Sir Kwingdale." Then Kwingdale set about the task of eating every nut in sight.

As the evil Sisters danced in the air, circling the wolf cub, they chanted.

> We are three sisters of the night
>
> Working to extinguish the Light.
>
> With the help of this cub
>
> Evil shall replace all love.
>
> There is no more to say,
>
> Until that dark, evil day.
>
> When the Darkness will reach its power

Resulting in our triumphant hour.

And as the Sisters sang and circled the cub he grew weaker and weaker.

♦

CHAPTER 3 - ALFONSES BERRY DAY

The Riishi sat in his hut and projected his consciousness to different parts of the land. Daily he scanned his section of the cosmic reality and reflected the Light into every corner. In many ways he was simply a mirror. The Light did not originate with him nor could he tell it what to do. The Light had a life and vitality of its own.

In this way the Riishi kept track of Turtle, Nerge, Kwingdale, the Sisters of Yor, the wolf cub and the mice of Berryville. By focusing the Light the Riishi perceived their need and could intercede as Directed. In time the Riishi would know what to do and when to act.

And as the Riishi finished scanning the land he began to look back on his own life. How short it all seemed. Where did the time go? What had he accomplished with the few hours he was given?

And as the Riishi realized what he was doing he started to laugh. The old villain was at it again. That part of the mind never dies. The best that can be said is that it serves a purpose. It asks the question, but the answer, the lasting answer, must be perceived by another mode of consciousness. That part provides the real answers.

We came into this realm to draw closer to the Light or Truth. We draw closer by service to the Light and following the Path. One follows the Path with the help of a teacher. The earth is never without the teachers. To each community they are sent. Usually working anonymously; the teachers are a hidden treasure.

The Riishi refocused his gaze on the land and felt the elements in the stew coming together. Soon the players would know their roles and participate in the evolution of their community.

◆

Turtle continued swimming upriver. Soon he would have to rest. The body could only take so much then a price had to be paid. Everything was a fine balance and to change the balance was to court danger. How many times had he given this lesson to young turtles; probably hundreds of times?

Often young turtles want to spend every moment catching silver minnows. They reason if one hour of practice was good then ten hours must be ten times better. Yet Turtles were much more than silver minnow catchers. In fact, the best were those who moderated their attention to this skill. It was not just a matter of effort. Effort had to be extended at the right time and place and in the correct circumstance. Turtles learned this through proper instruction and leading a balanced life.

What good was effort if it wasn't the proper time; when minnows were feeding? Or right place; their feeding ground? Or right circumstance; a genuine hunger? Few realized this. Successful effort was dependent upon linked factors. Particularly if one was searching for more than silver minnows.

For Turtle silver minnow catching was his bridge to the transcendent. By working in the world and performing everyday service as a teacher, Turtle experienced Truth. By focusing on the movement of a silver minnow's tail, Turtle learned to see past the world of appearances and perceive Reality. This was the hidden teaching which had been passed on in his family for generations. Occasionally a young turtle would attend his class and want something more. At first this youngster might be drawn to his class because it was an approved area for turtle education. Yet in those special students, Turtle perceived their inner call. It was his responsibility to awaken and nurture it.

For most turtles, silver minnow catching was a vocational skill; it helped them care for themselves and their family. For others it was the way they could connect with the inner reality and understand their place in the cosmic plan.

Turtle pushed on and promised himself he would stop in a few minutes.

In Berryville all the mice were anticipating the upcoming celebration. In one more week it was Alfonses' Berry Day. Alfonses' Day was always the second Tuesday in May. Legend has it this was the day the Great Mouse led Alfonses into the Widener Valley and Alfonses founded Berryville.

Alfonses had been out hunting for berries and got lost. Some versions of the story suggest Alfonses fell, hit his head on a granite stone thereby losing his memory for a time. Those who ascribe to this version tend to wear necklaces of small round granites believing the stones bring good luck.

One morning in his wanderings, Alfonses woke up and found himself surrounded by berry bushes. Alfonses decided to camp in the Valley and rest. Eventually when his memory returned, he moved all of his brothers and sisters to the Valley. The original founders took the name of Berry. Hence the mouse community was referred to as Berryville.

The Widener Valley which is home to Berryville derives its name from the wide entrance into the Valley. As mice regularly travel from community to community, the wide Valley mouth allows for safe passage.

Alfonses Day is known across the land and mice journey for weeks to participate in the festival. This is one of the most joyous days in mouse society. Some of the activities include: a beauty contest, a berry eating challenge, an evening of Songs to the Great Mouse and a water parade depicting the discoveries of Alfonses Berry.

Little did any of the mice realize that this year other events were planned which would change their lives forever.

♦

After a long day of overeating, Nerge and Kwingdale were stuffed and seated in their burrow. Both had consumed twice the mouse amount and looked like round fluffy balls.

Nerge turned toward Kwingdale and offered, "Why do we do this? We know overeating is not good for us yet we do it anyway. You like nuts and I eat berries and we just can't stop ourselves."

Kwingdale thought for a second then replied, "I don't know about you, but I do it because it's exciting. Eating nuts is fun and laying here stuffed is better than being bored. At least I had something I liked and quieted my hunger."

Nerge considered Kwingdale's reply: "Quieted his hunger... hum. What hunger really needed quieting? Then it hit Nerge. Was this seemingly unstoppable hunger for nuts and berries really an extension of our incompleteness? Was the primal hunger for the Great Mouse somehow converted into an exaggerated need for nuts and berries? Not possible or was it?"

Certainly he and Kwingdale had known mice that were taken over by their cravings for berries and nuts. This hunger ruled their life. Intellectually, Nerge always felt they were substituting one hunger for another. He could see this in those unfortunates but was this true, on a smaller scale, for himself and Kwingdale? Occasionally, he and Kwingdale went on these binges. Could they be substituting a lower hunger for a higher one?

Turtle stopped swimming and slowly climbed out of the water. He didn't know how many more days he would have to keep this up. Turtle wasn't a particularly fast swimmer but he was a strong one. He wasn't worried about the distance. Somehow he would know when he had gone far enough. The inner voice would tell him.

As a youth, Turtle spent hours swimming around the pond. Often this was the only way he could work off his inner turmoil. Turtle was one of those who never really fit in with the others. On the surface he looked like every other turtle. He loved to swim, catch minnows and make fun of the girl turtles. Yet there was an inner restlessness which would reappear. For years Turtle eased this restlessness by going off alone and swimming himself into exhaustion. This seemed to work until the next time.

As the years passed, Turtle learned to define this inner unease and hunger. It was a spiritual emptiness that only could be filled through silver minnow catching and the experience of Truth. Turtle went through many dark hours, until he was able to figure this out. When the unease could not be filled by swimming and there were times when this was certainly the case, Turtle would turn to some of the now legendary pursuits of his for fame and fortune.

By now surely everyone has heard the story of how Turtle wanted to become a world-famous diver and put on an exhibition to accomplish this?

Or the time Turtle sought fame as the mountain climbing turtle. Each time, Turtle put up signs announcing the fabulous deeds he was going to accomplish. A crowd gathered to watch and each time he got more than what he bargained for. In the diving exhibition Turtle actually dove off a high rock but no one believed it was him. The mountain climbing turtle never got off the ground so to speak. Turtle never lived either of these exploits down.

In time Turtle found inner peace and spiritual realization as a teacher of silver minnow catching. In his family this vocation was passed down through generations. Turtle merely assumed the duties that were waiting for him.

Enough thinking about the past; Turtle was cold and hungry. He turned his attention to more important things like dinner. Let's see if the famous teacher can catch his own dinner. Turtle began focusing upon the brown minnow that was swimming just off shore.

◆

As the wolf cub neared death he called out from the center of his soul. "Is there no one to help me?" This plea was barely audible. If another had been present they might not even have heard it. Yet to the dying cub it seemed like a scream.

Suddenly through foggy eyes the cub saw his mother. She had heard him. But how was that possible? Then the cub passed on to that place between life and death; that place where the soul makes its decision about which direction it will travel; will it go back to inhabit the body or travel onto the next place?

And as the cub considered the direction of travel, he remembered, I can't leave my mother. She might be hurt from the rock slide. This thought brought the cub's soul back to his weakened body with increased energy and purpose for life. When the cub opened his eyes, his mother was waiting with some fresh herbs for him to eat.

How could the cub know the Sisters of Yor, as energy forms, had the capacity to change at will? In choosing his mother, the cub was deceived into selecting the Darkness. The first part of the Prophecy was fulfilled.

◆

CHAPTER 4 - NERGE & KWINGDALE GO ON VACATION

One with the Light, the Riishi sat deep in meditation. As he continued to focus and reflect the Light, the Riishi began to pick up thought patterns. Slowly he recognized them as belonging to Nerge and Kwingdale.

The two mice were trapped in their pattern of excitement and overeating. Both were beginning to realize there might be something limiting with this behavior. This was the first step: recognizing the problem. Once the problem was defined, thought the Riishi, they might look for an answer.

On a physical level the answer was obvious, don't eat as much. On a spiritual level, it was more complex. For Nerge and Kwingdale this problem was an extension of their lack of spiritual completion and not eating as much would be a temporary solution.

Ultimately this conflict could only be resolved when the spiritual hunger was stilled. Until then the danger was ever present; even if they managed to stop overeating their primal emptiness would find another way to manifest. This hunger could only be quieted by the Light; the Light had to work in its own time and heal the soul.

And as the Riishi continued to reflect the Light, Nerge and Kwingdale fell asleep. It was a deep, peaceful sleep in which they dreamed of their youth in Berryville. They saw the mouse community and saw themselves as youngsters participating in the Alfonses Day celebration.

Later in the afternoon when they both awoke, Nerge and Kwingdale shared their dreams and took the coincidence as a sign from the Great Mouse. It was a week's journey, but both mice were excited about returning to Berryville for the yearly celebration.

◆

The Sisters of Yor combined their powers to assume the form of the cub's mother. As interdimensional travelers, assuming a physical form could not be maintained indefinitely. By concentrating in this manner, the Sisters reduced the range of their individual power and expended a tremendous amount of energy. In time this energy would become depleted and the Sisters would have to return to Yor and recharge, as it were. The rays of their dark sun were the source of life energy. In earth time this recharging took 100 years and they could not reenter the earth plane until it was completed.

Through the form of she-wolf, the Sisters worked as one. Understanding their time was limited, the Sisters focused on the cub. What had been missing was a reason to live. The reappearance of his mother was what he needed. Although extremely weak, the cub chewed some of the herbs and was beginning to feel stronger.

In a few days the Sisters hoped the cub would be strong enough to participate in the next phase of their plan.

◆

Until recently this journey upriver was something Turtle would have thought impossible. All turtles know how difficult it is to swim against the current and to swim for days this way, most believed couldn't be done. Yet Turtle conquered this problem by swimming deep below the surface. Most choose to swim on the surface, thought Turtle, and are unaware of the still water below. Turtles are complex and capable of all kinds of things; they just have to open themselves to the possibilities.

From time to time Turtle boxed himself into fixed thought and behavior patterns. Like others he was taught to think in a particular way and to want certain things. Each turtle had to fit into turtle and pond society. But what if a turtle wanted something different? It was possible, but there was always a price to pay.

For example, in Turtle's world, it was assumed you lived and died in the pond of your birth. A journey that Turtle was currently engaged in was unheard of for turtles. It was taught in turtle schools, if the Great Turtle wanted a turtle in another pond that turtle would have been born there. Everyone Turtle knew believed this as truth. Along with this view came the expectation that everything you needed was to be found in your pond. Turtles married other turtles they swam with as youngsters, and ate whatever was available in local waters.

Although an ancient profession, silver minnow catching and its teaching were evolutionary. Silver minnow catching taught many things and at its highest level asserted there was a world beyond the world of pond. Silver minnows, while an excellent source of food, also provided a way to Truth. Turtle knew if you could experience your transcendent nature, then, there had to be a world beyond the pond. The notion that something existed beyond pond frightened most turtles. That was why this inner doctrine and the method to realize it were kept a secret and shared with few.

It wasn't that this doctrine was unnatural; it was simply another way of looking at things. In years past many felt this view challenged society and their place in it. Yet these turtles closed themselves to the greater possibility. This transcendent view of the pond, helped in everyday affairs. It was a natural way to see past the world of forms and perceive the hidden patterns which were emerging.

When a turtle used his/her transcendent nature for others, he was better able to serve in the turtle world. How could Turtle explain to another, who didn't accept this expanded view, why he was on this journey? First, turtles didn't leave their ponds. Second, most were unaware of their intuitive powers. So if Turtle told another, "I am swimming upriver, against the current, because I have been ordered by my higher consciousness to go on this journey," that turtle would have called the turtle medics and sent Turtle away for a long, quiet, rest cure. Yet that was the way it was.

Turtle knew he had to go on a journey, but he did not know why or for how long? Also Turtle knew he would get a message to stop when it was time and to act when he must. That was the way the things worked. He didn't make the rules. His higher consciousness did.

♦

Nerge and Kwingdale prepared for their journey to Berryville. It had been five years since they left and made their home beneath the oak, beside the road, next to the field.

As Nerge helped Kwingdale push pebbles in front of their burrow, one of the stones seemed to sparkle in the sunlight, like a jewel. A jewel, this reminded Nerge of the story he heard as a youngster. Surely everyone who grew up in Berryville knew it.

'Once there was an old, wise Mouse King who had a very young son. This old King was afraid that after his death, the evil courtiers would try and steal the Prince's birthright. So the wise King hid treasure in a place where he knew that only the son would find it. This treasure included the biggest jewel anyone had ever seen. There the treasure remained; waiting for the son to claim his inheritance when he came of age.'

Was this one of the lost jewels? Ha! Ha! It was only a legend and Nerge pushed another pebble in front of their burrow.

♦

As Turtle prepared to go to sleep for the evening, he closed his eyes and began to focus on the inner reality. Slowly he put away his conscious desires and began to perceive the hidden world. As the inner eye began to open, Turtle felt at peace with his journey and at peace with the world.

Gone were all his doubts and desires. Gone was the world of the senses; there was only the Light, the Great Turtle and Turtle's higher consciousness. And as Turtle's consciousness joined with the Light he fell asleep.

♦

CHAPTER 5 - THE STORM RAGES

The Riishi sat on a hill that was covered with multi-colored wild flowers; they were yellow, white, purple, blue and pink. As he looked out across the meadow and the quiet valley, a dark rain cloud began to obscure the sun. A moment ago it was sunny. Now the sunlight was replaced by darkness. As the cloud moved closer, the Riishi began to feel rain drops against his face.

And as the Riishi watched the storm he began to compare the changing weather to his own personality. One moment he could feel happy and calm; the next full of anger. In the past the smallest thing could change the panorama of his mind. As the situation requires, each person is made up of a variety of faces, changing and mixing. The thing we call our personality is a kaleidoscope of moods, thoughts and desires. Forever shifting like the weather against this hill yet on an inner level each personality can be unified and one. The journey is to experience this Oneness and use this Unity to help others.

As the rain continued to fall, the Riishi walked back to his hut. In another hour the storm will have passed, the flowers will have drunk of the rain and the weather will change again. This view from the hill, while appearing unchanged for centuries, was forever evolving and so were we. From this form we will take on another and another, until we find our way back to the Source. We are the prodigal son who must return and in each realm, we draw a little closer by doing the work for which we were created.

So many travelers spend years trying to find themselves; trying to cultivate their own individuality. Yet there is something more lasting which is beyond personality and its shifting pattern. This is the object of the search. Not the endless traits which we take to be our personality. These traits are like colored shirts that we wear; each a little different but still a shirt. The spiritual traveler is interested in what lies beyond personality.

Many travelers are deceived by the notion they have to examine and change every aspect of their mind and personality. What is important to learn is there is awareness beyond what we take to be our personality. This is the essential self and is the part which will lead us into the next part of our journey.

Personality may be compared to a coat which is made up of many patches. Each patch is individual and distinctive yet the patches combine to form the entire garment. While the garment may be required for warmth and protection, there are times when it must be shed.

Similarly the various parts of our personality serve a function yet at times must be pushed aside. As you do not have to examine each patch to wear the coat nor do you have to dwell on each facet of your mind for it to work. These traits all serve a purpose but you must learn to look past them.

Also one must not dismiss the personality as being unimportant. A balance must be struck. We were created with talents and needs to express and must honor them in our journey. Like the patches on an old coat, they work together, but at the right time, the coat must be exchanged for another garment.

◆

Nerge and Kwingdale were arguing. Nerge wanted to take the road back to Berryville; he felt it was the shortest route. Along the way Kwingdale wanted to go through the forest and visit some of his friends. They had reached an impasse.

Nerge shouted at Kwingdale, "You are always trying to decide things for me! Why can't we ever do what I want? Why do we always have to do things your way?"

Kwingdale paused for a moment and replied, "All I was trying to say is that it might be more enjoyable if we stopped and visited some friends. I wasn't trying to boss you around."

Nerge continued, "Well I'm sick and tired of your bossiness and not budging until you agree to my plan."

Kwingdale seeing he wasn't getting anyplace, slowly pushed aside some of the pebbles from the burrow entrance, went back inside and lay down.

Nerge stood outside and continued shouting, "I'm not moving until you agree to take the road back to Berryville!"

That night Nerge slept outside their burrow and Kwingdale stayed inside.

♦

As the storm raged the Sisters shielded the cub with their body from the driving rain. As he rested against his mother's side, the cub was unafraid. Let the rain fall, thought the cub, I have my mother to protect me. She must have been injured by the rocks. That's why it took her so long to find me. Look, I can see where the cuts have healed into a scar. The cub lay beside his mother, smiled and went back to sleep.

The Sisters were almost ready to teach the cub to kill for enjoyment. He had started to eat wild game again. The Sisters realized the cub wasn't strong enough and it would be a matter of days before he could hunt for himself. The cub's mother had taught him to kill because it was necessary. What the evil Sisters planned was unnatural. It defied the natural order of things and would lead the cub closer to the Darkness; and as the Darkness grew their plan moved forward.

◆

In the morning when Nerge and Kwingdale awoke their argument was a faint memory. Both were embarrassed. They apologized to each other and compromised by following the river back to Berryville.

◆

Due to the heavy rain the preparations for Alfonses Day were brought indoors. Under the supervision of their parents, the young mice who were in the beauty contest and water pageant practiced inside their burrows. Little had changed over the years and the older mice easily showed the youngsters what they had to do. Each of the youngsters were honored to be part of the formal festivities and concentrated on their roles.

And as the rain continued to fall, grasses and trees drank of the water, growing green and full. In the last few days Berryville had become a bouquet of flowers and wild berries. All the mouse elders happily anticipated the celebration. It had been years since Berryville looked so lush and full of life. Everyone felt this was to be a celebration to remember.

◆

CHAPTER 6 - MUD SLIDE

When Turtle awoke he was covered with mud. The heavy rains washed a small, adjacent hillside down on top of him. Amazingly Turtle slept through the entire thing. He had been exhausted. And as he slept Turtle was aware of being wet but he thought he was still swimming and went back to sleep.

As the sun came up the mud started to cake and Turtle could barely move. How Turtle hated mud! It made him feel dirty and slimy. If the mud completely dried he would be trapped. It was not uncommon for turtles to die this way.

Suddenly Turtle's adrenaline began to flow and he started kicking to free himself. These quick movements caused him to sink deeper into the mud. The more Turtle thrashed about the more dangerous the situation became. What had been a problem at first, now bordered on becoming a catastrophe.

Then Turtle heard the inner command, "Be still and think." As Turtle lay almost completed covered with mud, he focused his thoughts inward and started to sort out the problem. By kicking wildly, Turtle made the situation desperate; perhaps if he had moved in small, measured amounts, he may have been able to free himself. Instead he became frightened, acted emotionally and created a potentially deadly situation.

As Turtle lay still, inside his shell, he remembered turtles could survive for days if they had access to fresh air. Slowly Turtle inched his head out of the shell. He closed his eyes and began pushing the mud with his nose. Fortunately with just a little pressure he was able to get part of his head out of the mud. At this point near his head the mud was not very thick. Next, Turtle took a deep breath and slowly worked his way back into his shell. By moving his head in and out, Turtle was able to create a breathing hole. This took a few minutes. Then Turtle took some time to rest and decide what to do next.

And as Turtle thought about his predicament and responsibilities, he began to sob. Wasn't he on a journey for the Great Turtle? Was this the way it was going to end? Turtle felt sorry for himself and the real mess he was in. As the tears continued they washed away most of the mud from his eyes and face. Sobbing on and on, Turtle began to realize he could see. Also he could stick his head out of his shell and mud. If he could do this then there was hope. Sooner or later someone might find him. After all he could live like this for days.

He had just eaten and drank plenty of water while swimming. He had air and could call for help to travelers along the river.

There was hope. He was not forgotten!

◆

Nerge and Kwingdale were walking along the river bank and growing tired. They had been traveling nonstop for hours. Both were hungry and irritable. As they were in a hurry to reach Berryville both agreed to keep going despite the rain.

Walking along the river they shared stories of the past. Nerge said to Kwingdale. "Do you remember the time you tried out for the lead in the Alfonses Day Pageant? You wanted to be Alfonses Berry so badly because that cute, little girl mouse, what was her name, was going to be the female lead?"

"I remember the tryouts as if they yesterday. Her name was Estelle and I had a huge crush on her. For days I memorized my lines. When it was time for Alfonses to kiss his sweetheart goodbye, I froze. I couldn't kiss Estelle in front of everyone so I pretended I was ill and ran from the stage. Everyone laughed and called me the running mouse. I really sprinted that day.

"Do you remember when we were playing beneath the oak tree? You got hit in the head with an acorn and were knocked unconscious? When you awoke you wanted to make your life a study of nuts and why they fell from trees. You thought this was the most important thing you could do. You wanted to save others from the misfortune you suffered so you drew and studied oak and nut angles for weeks. You even prepared a short paper to deliver before the Berryville Scientific Society. When you presented your paper to the Society President he replied:

'Mr. Nerge the dangers of falling acorns have been recorded in our journals for years. If you would have taken the time to ask, we could have saved you a great deal of time and energy. In fact the whole matter can be summarized by the well know saying. "Watch out for falling nuts unless you want to get cracked.'

Certainly you made yourself into a laughing stock that day."

While the two friends shared stories, they forgot how tired they were. Somehow laughter made traveling easier.

♦

Every five to ten minutes, Turtle stuck his head out of his shell to see if any travelers were close enough to help. As Turtle strained to listen, he heard a faint, muffled sound. It sounded as if someone were laughing. Yes that's it. More than one traveler was walking along the river bank and they were laughing.

Relieved and realizing he might be saved, Turtle began to laugh uncontrollably; and he laughed and laughed. Finally he regained his composure and listened to make sure the travelers were still approaching. They were! Turtle called out, "Help me! Help me! I am stuck. Help me!"

♦

When they heard Turtle, Nerge and Kwingdale stopped to listen. At first they couldn't tell the direction. But as they concentrated, gradually they determined the calls were coming from directly in front of them. When they realized someone was in danger, Nerge and Kwingdale started to run to help.

As they turned at the bend in the river, Nerge spotted the mud pile. Nerge whispered to Kwingdale, "The calls are coming from that pile of mud. You know how sneaky thieves can be." Kwingdale replied, "Come on, we have to see if someone is hurt. In case it's a trap, let's sneak up."

♦

Turtle was facing upriver and the laughter was coming from his rear. From their sounds, Turtle couldn't tell anything about the travelers. All he knew was someone or something was approaching. He had no way to tell if the travelers were friendly. Turtle was growing desperate. What had he to lose? So he kept on yelling. "Help me! Help me!" If he was going to die before fulfilling his mission, it might as well be here, now. "Help me! Help me!"

♦

Cautiously Nerge and Kwingdale approached the pile of mud. From their position, all they could see was a large, brown heap with a head sticking out of it. The head was yelling for help.

Simultaneously Nerge and Kwingdale wondered what type of creature they were facing. They had never encountered anything quite like this. A mole or a mouse lived underground and were not that large. Then Nerge thought out loud, "Perhaps there are two animals in the mud. The bigger creature that is hidden is pulling the smaller underground. The head sort of looks like a lizard and the brown heap looks like a snake. That's it. A large snake is pulling a lizard into its hole."

Kwingdale said to Nerge, "I think you're right. Come on we have to save our brother the lizard." Meanwhile Turtle was getting frantic and kept shouting. "Help me! Help me!"

This shouting made Nerge and Kwingdale even more nervous. Kwingdale said, "This is our plan. I will get a stick and use it on the snake. While I am poking the snake, you go over and pull the lizard out of the hole."

Nerge gave Kwingdale a couple of seconds to find a stick then the two mice charged the mud pile. At a furious rate, Kwingdale began hitting the mud and Turtle started yelling louder because of the blows. Nerge took Turtle's screams as a sign that things were getting desperate.

So Nerge yanked hard on Turtle's head, hoping to pull the lizard out of the snake's grasp. As Kwingdale poked and Nerge yanked, Turtle wondered what was going on. Exasperated and stunned, Turtle screamed, "Stop it! What are you two fools trying to do, kill me?" Frightened, Nerge let go of Turtle's head but Kwingdale kept poking away. Finally gathering every bit of self-control that he could muster, Turtle said to Nerge, "Will you tell your friend to stop hitting me. I am turning black and blue."

When Nerge realized that it was one creature beneath the mud, Nerge shouted to Kwingdale, "Stop it! We are hurting him."

"Hurting who?" asked Kwingdale.

"I don't know but he said to stop it."

Kwingdale stopped poking and after a few awkward moments, everything was straightened out.

Later after hours of digging, Turtle was freed. He was sore and bruised but free. While Turtle went for a swim and soaked his battered body, Nerge and Kwingdale sat on the shore and rested.

As Turtle cleaned himself in the water, Nerge called out, "How did you happen to find yourself in this mess?"

Turtle replied, "Do you want the long or short version?"

"I'll take the short."

"Just as I figured. Well, I am on a journey and I stopped to rest. When I awoke, I was covered with mud."

"Why didn't you just climb out?"

"I tried to do that but every time I moved, I got in deeper."

"You said you were on a journey. What a coincidence so are we. Where are you headed?" inquired Kwingdale.

"I'm heading upriver," said Turtle.

"How far are you going?" asked Nerge.

"I really don't know."

"Let me get this straight. You're on a journey upriver and you don't know how far. What kind of journey is that?"

"That's sort of correct. You see I know the direction but not the distance. When I need them, I'll get the orders to stop."

"Who do you get your orders from?"

Turtle replied, "From the Great Turtle."

Nerge mumbled to himself, "From the Great Turtle. Hmm... we've got a live one here. Better not tell him where we are going."

While Turtle continued to float in the river, Nerge whispered to Kwingdale, "Let's dump this turtle as soon as we can. I don't think all the pieces fit together. He thinks he's on a mission for the Great Turtle. Who is this Great Turtle, anyway?"

That night while Turtle slept, Nerge and Kwingdale snuck off into the woods. Both were afraid that while they slept, the Great Turtle might order Turtle to eat two mice. They wanted none of this.

In the morning, when Turtle awoke he saw that Nerge and Kwingdale were gone. He assumed they had gotten up early to continue their journey. Turtle wondered why they hadn't said goodbye and was a little hurt by this.

♦

The rain had stopped and the cub was feeling stronger. He stood and stretched his legs. Daily he could feel his muscles growing more powerful and knew soon he would be able to hunt for himself.

For now he was grateful his mother could help. She had just brought the remains of a rabbit for him to eat and he was hungry.

♦

CHAPTER 7 - SPIRITUAL ENERGY BOOST

As the Riishi focused the Light upon Berryville and the surrounding countryside, he saw the Plan coming together. All the elements were in motion and at the right moment would combine: Nerge and Kwingdale were traveling to Berryville, preparations were taking place for Alfonses Day, Turtle had been rescued and was again swimming upriver, and the Sisters of Yor were grooming the cub.

This coming together of the various elements was all part of the Design. In some ways it represented the primal act of creation and, as a result of this happening, the world of field mice and turtles would never be the same.

Before something can happen in the physical world there must be the right combination of factors- right time, right place, right participants- so it is on a spiritual level. In order for a personality to be transmuted, various elements must work together and combine. That part of the personality which is tied to the world remains, yet, is changed and knows when to step aside. In order for the Plan to operate both parts of the personality must work together. That is why one speaks of transmutation rather than elimination.

As the Light works on a personality so this happens to entire communities and potentially nations. This is the act of creation and is one of the functions of the Light.

Slowly the elements were moving toward Berryville. This was the Prophecy which had existed since the Beginning and carried far into the future. It was a continuum, with countless factors and variations leading to this time and place. On one level of reality this happening had always existed and would continue for centuries.

Then the Riishi focused his spiritual gaze toward the Center where the others joined daily. For this realm, this was the point of Origination and Power. Here the Riishi melded his consciousness with the other servants and became a ray of Light, shining Life and Love across the creation.

Turtle resumed his swimming upriver and for turtles was moving along at a terrific speed. The rescue by the two field mice reaffirmed Turtle's belief he was on a mission for the Great Turtle.

While the two mice seemed confused about Turtle's purpose, he was clear. This certainty came through years of experience. Often he felt the need to do things without understanding all the factors involved. It was an intuitive feeling and knowledge something had to be done. There was no examination of possibilities, you just knew it. This capacity to know, beyond everyday rational thought, was as natural to turtles as their shells. Because most turtles over-looked this possibility, it was never fully developed and lay dormant.

In silver minnow catching the best students were those who through concentration knew which way the minnow was going to swim. By focusing on the minnow, a student could become one with the fish and join his thoughts. Once this happened, the minnow was as good as eaten. The young turtle sensed how the fish would react. This experience of expanded consciousness opened the way for other experiences. With Turtle's assistance the young turtle was on the Path to knowing.

How could he explain this dimension of his life to the two mice? No wonder they left early. When Turtle said he was on a journey for the Great Turtle, they probably thought he was crazy. Ha! Ha!

♦

After their encounter with Turtle, Nerge and Kwingdale followed the forest path to Berryville. If they continued to follow the river path, they might run into Turtle again and wanted to avoid this possibility. As they walked, Kwingdale thought to himself, "If we had taken the forest to begin with none of this would have happened."

Kwingdale failed to realize, while they compromised because of an argument to follow the river, there was a spiritual purpose in all of this. If Kwingdale looked deeper he might have realized their presence saved Turtle's life.

While it was possible someone else might have assisted, they were the ones who did. What Kwingdale could not have known was their destinies would again entwine, and it was essential they meet before this happened.

♦

Turtle continued swimming upriver and found himself in a school of silver minnows. There were hundreds of them. The minnows seemed unafraid and continued on. Turtle did not have the time nor desire for a snack. Perhaps the minnows sensed this.

Then Turtle focused straight ahead and concentrated even harder on his strokes. Suddenly

Turtle found himself swimming among hundreds of Lights. And as Turtle's gaze remained fixed, his body continued swimming faster. And as he focused on the rays of Light, he saw them turn into young turtles. Within each of the turtles there was the same ray of Light and it was joined with the others to light up the water.

And as he continued swimming, he saw these rays of Light affix to a thousand different life events and experiences. Some turtles became parents, others divers and swimmers. Some lost themselves in a haze of despair and although dimmer their Light continued to shine. Then he saw hundreds of young turtles grow old and pass away from all kinds of things; some from predators, others by hunger and disease. Yet after death their Lights continued to shine. And as Turtle swam, the Lights turned into minnows, again.

Somehow turtles and silver minnows were connected. Turtle felt this way for many years and here was the answer. They were joined by the same Light of creation and had the same Creator. This ray of Light, while it could attach itself to any number of things, would never die. This ray was indestructible and yearned to rejoin the Light from which it came. That was the point of the journey: a reunion of Lights.

That was why turtles were born and died. That was why there were silver minnows. Each had a destiny, a journey of reunion. While the ray could attach itself to many things, it could only find lasting completion in its Source, the Light.

We were born incomplete, yearning for the moment of completion. And as Turtle's consciousness continued to expand, he found himself in an unfamiliar place. Turtle's body was still swimming upriver, but that part which was truly Turtle had gone someplace else.

And as Turtle looked around, he could see various beings of Light. Some had the form of turtles, others of field mice and still others of forms he did not recognize. Here everyone knew each other. No one spoke but all knew each other's thoughts. Each being of Light was connected in some beautiful, joyous way. Turtle felt truly at peace.

Then Turtle's body sent out a message, he was in trouble. His right, rear leg was suffering a cramp and Turtle had better get his ray of Light back into the shell or soon there would be another turtle on the river bottom for catfish to eat.

So Turtle's higher consciousness rejoined his suffering body and took care of some really important business, keeping alive.

♦

And as the Riishi continued reflecting the Light, he became the going out and coming in. He became the primordial ray of Light which was sent out into the Darkness to find its way home to the Creator. Then he became the Creator ready to welcome the Light home.

The Riishi traveled through both worlds and in each became both Darkness and Light. He saw on one level they were different, on another they were the same. Each had its function and each was created to serve.

Next the Riishi looked and saw the war between Darkness and Light alive in his own breast. For his daily existence he was dependent upon physical sensations yet on another level he was a child of light. While one part pulled toward the earth another pulled toward the heavens.

This was the way it was since the beginning when the original pact was signed. This was the struggle to which creatures of flesh were born. In order to draw closer, the battle must be waged. As it was in this realm so it was in others. The return was one of struggle and learning. Learn to see the Creator in all worlds and struggle to keep the Creator's Need foremost in mind.

The cosmic self or divine ray took on a physical form to draw closer to the Light. In so doing it became aware of its physical desires. To walk in this realm each must be concerned with their physical needs. When this concern becomes exaggerated it is a selfish concern. This selfishness pulls away from the Light and binds to the physical.

That aspect of the Universe which pulls away from the Light, again, manifested in the physical realm. The Sisters of Yor were the current emissaries of this pull toward selfishness. They wished to control the physical plane to glorify the Darkness. Fortunately other influences were at work to balance this pull. At the right moment, these factors would again come into play. His duty was to make sure all was in accord with the Plan.

♦

CHAPTER 8 - DECEPTION CONTINUES

Walking around the cub the Sisters began to discuss the next part of their Plan. "The cub is fond of rabbits but he must learn to like field mice. Then we can teach him to kill for sport. Once this is accomplished, he will be ready for Berryville."

When the cub was finished with the rabbit, the Sisters began, "Do you know why I was gone for so long? I was healing from a rock slide. As I lay close to death, some field mice from Berryville made fun of me. They would not help and taunted. "Look at the proud huntress, now, she has fallen and we are triumphant. We caused the rocks to fall and hoped to kill you. Now, we are going to let you die a slow death."

Shocked the cub inquired, "Mother, how did you manage to survive?"

"Fortunately I lay near some of the famous berries of Berryville. I taught myself to feed off those horrid things. While they tasted bitter remarkably there was enough nutrition and moisture to keep me alive. The healing took a long time and I was always afraid the mice would return to finish me. As I lay helpless, I made a vow should I live I would avenge myself.

"Yet as I filled with anger against my enemies, I knew my first responsibility was to find you. I knew you were not ready to be on your own and you could die without my help. So as soon as I could move I set out to find you. While those evil mice nearly killed me, they almost finished you as well."

And as the Sisters continued with their story, the cub began to feel anger growing in his heart. Never had the cub felt anything like this. As his mother continued to speak of her pain and suffering, the cub's anger turned into rage.

◆

Nerge and Kwingdale continued walking. Traveling the forest trail had pluses and minuses. Due to the recent rain, the forest floor was alive with spring flowers and plants. However this made progress very slow.

Nerge and Kwingdale were tired. As they stopped to rest, Nerge said to Kwingdale, "I feel the need to preach. Since we set out on this journey, I have not spoken about the Great Mouse and I feel the need to do so." Kwingdale replied, "Be my guest but I am stopping right here. Why don't you go over to those trees and see if you can find a listener."

So Nerge set out to find someone, anyone who might listen to what he had to say. As Nerge made his way to the nearby fir trees, he started to hear some talking. At first he couldn't make out the voices and was excited that he might find some fellow travelers to convert. But as he drew closer, the voices sounded dangerously like wolves.

Nerge slowed his pace and moved carefully toward the trees. If there were wolves close by he and Kwingdale had to be very cautious. So Nerge inched closer and when he reached the trees, he couldn't believe his eyes. There was a wolf cub who was talking to something which looked like a large wolf, but you could see right through it. It was much larger than the cub and didn't look like any wolf Nerge had ever seen. In fact, it sort of resembled a wolf spirit.

Suddenly Nerge got frightened and decided whatever was talking to the cub wasn't going to like his being there. All mice knew wolves generally didn't bother with them. Wolves considered field mice too tart because of their diet of berries and preferred rabbits. But who knew what spirits liked?

So Nerge turned around and slowly crept back to where Kwingdale was seated. As Nerge approached he whispered, "We better get out of here.

There are two wolves over by those trees." Without another word the two mice scampered out of that part of the forest.

♦

After running for 30 minutes they stopped and Nerge told Kwingdale what he had observed. Kwingdale listened without speaking until Nerge finished. Then Kwingdale offered, "I have never heard anything like this. It's a good thing you got us out of there. What if they had found us? We would be two dead mice. That's for sure." While saying these words Kwingdale didn't believe any of it and was thinking something else. "Poor Nerge he really has gone over the deep end. This trip back to Berryville really must have unsettled him."

Letting his cramp rest, Turtle lay on the river bank. And as he soaked his leg in some soothing river mud, he wondered what the extended spiritual experience meant. Whenever these states overcame him, it was a foretaste that something difficult was ahead. In fact these states were almost like a spiritual energy pep talk. This frightened Turtle. This had been a very strong experience. The last time something like this happened, young turtle lost his life. Young turtle was eaten by a copperhead and Turtle had been unable to help.

Remembering this incident, Turtle began to sweat. He looked out across the river. The river was calm and Turtle saw two dragonflies chasing each other. He followed their flight for a time and this relaxed him a bit. Then Turtle realized whatever it was, as the Great Turtle wished, he would do his best.

◆

It was morning. Turtle reentered the water and started upriver. These were unfamiliar waters and Turtle had to be on guard for water snakes. Perhaps this was what the spiritual state was warning him about?

As Turtle plodded along, suddenly, he got an urge to stop. Pulling himself out of the water, Turtle noticed the bushes along the river were filled with tiny, red berries. They were everywhere on all the river bushes and even those bushes which led into the forest. Admiring the berries, Turtle noticed a team of field mice loading them into sacks.

Turtle called out, "Friends, I am a stranger in these parts. Where am I and why are the bushes full of tiny berries?"

One of the young mice called back, "Have you never heard of Berryville? We are picking berries to help celebrate Alfonses Day. This celebration is scheduled to begin the day after tomorrow. Mice will be arriving from all over the land. Why don't you join us? Turtles are welcome."

"Thank you but I am on a journey and I am unsure where it will end. Otherwise I would be happy to join in. Tell me are these berries good to eat?"

"Well we mice like them. I don't know if they will suit a turtle's taste. Why don't you try one?"

Turtle picked one up and smelled it. Then he rolled it around and thought to himself, "It looks alright to me. Maybe it's a trick. Perhaps these mice are trying to trick me into eating something that will make me sick or even kill me?"

Then Turtle realized if he didn't eat the berry, the mice might get insulted and attack. There must be ten or 12 of them and they are all watching. "Boy I really got myself into a mess. Either way, I'm a goner. If I eat the berry, I'll probably die and if I don't the mice will make turtle soup out of me."

Turtle reasoned he couldn't make it to the river before the mice reached him and they looked like they were getting impatient. "Oh well, let me try one. If I don't like it, I can spit it out." So Turtle took a bite. Lo and behold, the berry was delicious and he didn't feel sick. Yet it could be one of those foods that take a few minutes for the poison to work. So Turtle smiled and called back, "This berry is delicious," while he considered his next move.

And as Turtle decided whether or not to take a second bite, the mice went back to work ignoring Turtle. When Turtle realized the berry wasn't poisonous and the mice were uninterested, Turtle turned around and went back into the river.

Swimming away and not feeling any effect of the berry, Turtle realized two bites were required for the poison to work. He considered himself lucky to have escaped; relieved he stopped after the first bite.

♦

Nerge and Kwingdale entered Widener Valley. It was as beautiful as they remembered. Ever since Alfonses Berry discovered this Valley, it had been a safe place for field mice to live. The Valley lay hidden many miles in the deep forest. Also the Valley mouth was extremely wide and if a stray wolf wandered into this area, he could easily be tracked and avoided. Sentries were posted and signaled each other until the hunter left. Usually this didn't take very long. There were few rabbits in the Valley and usually wolves were uninterested in mice.

The Valley, while famous for its entrance, was equally noted for its scenic and mountainous back end. Here the town of Berryville was situated. The town was lined by beautiful mountain peaks and a crystal clear lake lay at its feet. The citizens of Berryville drew water from Alfonses' Lake and swam in the river which ran through the Valley and fed the Lake.

When traveling to Berryville, due to the high peaks, most visitors walked through the Valley mouth. Few climbed the mountains anymore and it had been years since commercial traffic went across the mountains. While the early settlers were adept at climbing, recent generations felt this skill unnecessary. Hence all traffic entered through the Valley mouth and a sentry system ensured safe passage.

As Nerge and Kwingdale continued walking they were greeted by one of the sentries. She called out, "Visitors welcome to the Widener Valley, home of Alfonses Berry and our yearly celebration. Do you need a place to stay or do you have relatives here?"

Kwingdale called back, "We are two citizens of Berryville who left years ago and have returned for the celebration." With these words the sentry signaled them to pass. Nerge and Kwingdale were growing excited. In less than two hours, they would be in Berryville and planned to stay with Nerge's mother. Who hadn't seen her son in nearly five years.

♦

And as the Riishi observed the different players, he wondered how it would all end. While he was aware of the various influences and his own role, the Riishi did not know the outcome. This was not something that he needed to know; all he needed to know was how and when to act. This would be conveyed by the Light through his own sensitivity.

The Riishi used to think higher knowledge was something miraculous. He came to realize it was very natural. Within each creature there was the capacity to be one with the Light. For some it took years of work but it was natural. After all a turtle did not learn to swim in just one lesson; it took hours to master the different currents and water temperature. On a spiritual level, it was similar with spiritual learning.

Then the Riishi felt a disruption in the Light. It was coming from Berryville. Instantly the Riishi understood the Sisters were putting in motion the second phase of the Prophecy.

◆

CHAPTER 9 - KILLING FOR FUN

The young cub questioned, "Where are we going? Why are we walking toward the Widener Valley? Everyone knows there are no rabbits there."

The Sisters, in the form of the she-wolf, replied, "I have told you. I was injured in the Widener Valley and there is some business I must take care of."

Cautiously the two wolves slipped into the Valley. They were careful to avoid the sentries. All the while, the cub wondered why they were there.

Suddenly the she-wolf signaled the cub to stop. She began creeping toward a small group of rocks. The cub could hear faint sounds coming from that direction. Next the she-wolf leaped to the top of the rocks, paused for an instant then jumped. In a matter of seconds it was all over and the she-wolf gripped two dead field mice in her jaws. These she carried to the cub and dropped at his feet.

With a grin on her face, she offered, "Come taste the sweetness of revenge. Now we will see who is laughing."

And as the cub looked down at the dead field mice and his smiling mother, sadness came over him. "This is wrong yet my mother smiles," thought the cub. "How can this be? She taught me to kill only for survival. Now she kills and enjoys it."

Almost as if she could read his mind, the she-wolf offered, "Little one, do not think badly of me. This is a form of survival. Field mice left me to die. By leaving me in the cold, badly injured, did they try not to kill me? I am only protecting myself and you. They might try to attack again."

And as the cub listened to his mother, he thought, "She is right." Yet as he agreed with her and stared at the dead mice, his sadness grew.

Finally Nerge and Kwingdale reached Berryville. Berryville was bright with all the colors of spring and decorated with large murals depicting the exploits of Alfonses Berry. Quickly Nerge walked toward his mother's burrow and questions filled his mind. "Will she be there? I have not written in two years. Will I be welcome? Does she still love me?"

Hesitantly he stepped up to the opening of the burrow and called inside, "Mother are you home? It's me, Nerge. Kwingdale and I are here for a visit."

From inside came a soft sweet voice, "Nerge, is that really you? Quickly, come inside. I have missed you!"

◆

Continuing to reflect the Light, the Riishi reminisced about the past. "Yes, the winds of change were blowing across Berryville, like those that had blown across my life. When I was young, I was convinced that I was master of my fate. After the Light worked on my heart, I realized what I considered my personality was nothing more than a product of my environment and inborn need. As I was raised in a certain village, at a particular time and place, so I was influenced by specific social factors and taught to want certain things. What I considered my personality was nothing more than a series of natural biological, emotional and societal tendencies and desires created by others.

"As I searched for the real me, I found this center very elusive. Some parts of me wanted this thing or that, but what lay beyond these wants and desires I had no idea. Initially, I thought these wants and desires were all of who I was. At the time, I failed to realize that I was not fully equipped to make the inner search. I was searching for what lay beyond my desires and I had no way to proceed. Also if I found an answer, I had no way to evaluate it.

"Coincidently as I was framing these questions, the Master came into my life. One night, as I was dreaming, he appeared to me and questioned, "Are you asleep or awake? Are you dead or alive? Seek Truth and you will have your answers. Seek the world and you will have nothing."

'These words frightened me and I bolted awake. From that night forward, my life has not been the same. For many years, nightly in my dreams, the Master visited and instructed me in the Path to completion. He reflected the Light upon my heart, until I was strong enough to seek the Light on my own. Then the Master left.

"Just as the Master directed the Light toward me so I direct it toward others. The Light is the enabling factor and is the very fabric of the universe. It is a life giving nutrient which brings out what is latent in an organism; without the Light, life would cease."

And as the Riishi reflected the Light toward Berryville, he could feel the change. Slowly the Riishi realized anew the change would affect him as well.

♦

Turtle continued swimming against the current and was growing tired. Although he was in deep water and the current was weak at this level, his leg ached. As Turtle focused ahead, fighting the pain, he perceived a change in the current. Turtle swam a little further and realized he was at a fork in the river. If he went left he would have to fight the current. If he went right, he could glide along. This was an easy decision. Turtle made a right turn.

◆

Now two wolves staked the mouth of the Valley. Before this day ended, the she-wolf hoped to complete the second phase of the Prophecy. Each time they came upon a sentry mouse, the she-wolf killed and placed it at the cub's feet. Still the cub refused to join the hunt.

Finally she realized she had to force the cub's participation. So she stopped walking and began to cry.

"Mother why are you weeping?" inquired the cub.

In a faint, sobbing voice she replied, "Because you do not help me. Don't you love me?"

"Of course I love you but I am afraid. I have never killed or eaten a field mouse before. I am not sure it is the right thing to do. Usually wolves eat rabbits."

Again the she wolf picked up the dead mouse in her mouth and placed at the cub's feet offering, "How can it be wrong to help your mother?"

Reluctantly the cub picked up the mouse with his teeth. And as he tasted the warm, sweet flesh, the cub forgot about right and wrong. All he could think about was the sweetness of the mouse's blood and revenge.

Later as the cub joined the hunt, phase two of the Prophecy was completed.

♦

CHAPTER 10 - SEEING THE FUTURE?

Gliding along with the current, Turtle felt the river getting shallower. He had seen this type of flow before and knew from experience; either it would end up in a lake or slow trickle that died out. When it happened, he would deal with either situation.

From experience Turtle learned not to expect anything. While he mentally prepared for either eventuality, it was best not to spend time wondering what was going to happen. He had to focus. It was best just to react and use his energy on the actual situation.

The most difficult thing for Turtle to learn had been to see reality or what was actually occurring. Often he would cloud a situation with his own wants and expectations. Clearly the river had turned into a strong stream and would end soon. Why use mental energy worrying what would happen next? He was better off using his energy to navigate and focus.

It was easy to work-up a scenario, in his mind, how the stream would end and what he would do when this happened. It was exciting to think about all the possibilities. Yet this was usually unproductive. Usually the reality of a situation was far different than what Turtle pictured.

Some turtles became frozen by their fantasies and fears. In silver minnow class he would point this out to young turtles. The first obstacle was to overcome the excitement cycle. Most turtles became attracted to silver minnow catching because it was exciting. A turtle could gain fame catching silver minnows; he had seen it many times. Yet as some turtles sat on the rocks waiting for their moment to strike they became frozen with fear.

Instead of focusing on the minnow, thoughts about failure and success entered their mind. While either was a realistic possibility, it was not something to consider while you were trying to catch minnows. You were supposed to focus and become one with the minnow.

The objective was not to destroy these patterned thoughts; often they were useful and could be built upon. If the student used his fear to become a better hunter, it was productive up to a point to worry about minnow catching. One of the techniques silver minnow catching tried to teach was how to push these thoughts aside for a time and let the higher consciousness emerge and master the situation. By becoming one with the situation, a turtle could triumph over minnows and his own fear and desire.

Thinking about success or failure when one should be focusing on the minnow's tail was unproductive. The turtle had to brush these thoughts aside.

"There I go again," thought Turtle. I have let my mind wander over all kinds of things, when I should be watching the stream. This also happens in older Turtles.

Nerge's mother was happy to see her son and Kwingdale. It had been five years since they were together in Berryville. While their visit was a surprise, in a way, she had expected it and recalled her dream.

'The three of them were sitting in her burrow and talking about the past. This was the pleasant part and easiest to understand. The frightening part was all the blood and confusion. As she sat talking with Nerge and Kwingdale, they started bleeding from their throats. When this happened they cried out, "Wolves. Wolves!"

The next part was even more difficult to follow. Nerge was lying on the ground bleeding from his throat, yet speaking. He was saying, "I have returned to serve and must die to do so." Similarly Kwingdale was saying, "In every community there are those who can lead."

The most confusing part was seeing a turtle, a giant turtle rise up from Alfonses Lake. He just stood on the water smiling and as he smiled, he turned into a beautiful jewel. It was the most beautiful jewel she had ever seen; as the sunlight reflected through the jewel, the Light sparkled all over Berryville. When the Light hit upon Nerge and Kwingdale, miraculously their wounds were healed.'

While the old mouse affectionately looked at her son and his friend, she thought, "Enough of dreams. Who can understand them anyway? I have my son home and am the luckiest mouse in Berryville."

♦

The Riishi continued to reflect the Light to Turtle, Nerge, Kwingdale, the mice of Berryville and the cub. As the Light worked on their souls, it helped ready them for what lay ahead. On a spiritual level they were being prepared for the next phase in the Plan. While their conscious mind might balk at the possibility, their inner awareness recognized and bowed to it.

There was a part of all creatures that was hidden and could be awakened under the proper circumstance. It was this Reality the Light communicated with. So important was this aspect, that if it were removed, the creature would cease to exist. In fact this was the part that leads them into this world and would lead them to the next place. Some called this center, the spiritual heart.

While the Riishi could perceive how events might transpire, it was not his place to interfere. Within certain limits each must make their own decision. While the Prophecy had been written and was part of the Plan, each player must choose to do their part.

This was the concept of Design and early on had been difficult for the Riishi to accept. If the Light knew how the Plan must proceed, then why give choices? If players could not deviate beyond certain limits? Why go through the whole thing?

And the Riishi laughed. The old villain was still working in his mind; even after all these years. It was simple. In the process, learning was to occur. As Turtle, Nerge, Kwingdale and the cub made their decisions they changed. Free will choice was their birthright. Part of the Design was to allow this to happen. In the process, the alchemy would take place. Berryville and its inhabitants would change and be taken to the next level of their development.

And as this occurred in this world so it occurred in others. Until the journey home was complete. All along the way there were opportunities to embrace the Light. So if a creature failed to embrace the Light in this world because it was not their time, there would be other opportunities to understand the purpose of the journey. It was a journey of Love and Light with countless opportunity.

♦

Having killed all the valley sentries, the two wolves approached Berryville; where all the field mice were gathering beside Alfonses Lake. It was Alfonses Day. The ceremonies were beginning with a parade of water floats. Each of the floats was designed to depict an event in the life of Alfonses Berry and was operated by a team of rowers; while one of the entrants in the Beauty Pageant waived to onlookers. This was the day of days. Everyone was beside the Lake enjoying the fun.

Traveling beside the cub, the Sisters of Yor began to focus their inner gaze upon the Darkness. Slowly them emptied themselves of personal thought and let the Darkness fill them. And as the Darkness began to possess their souls, they became one with It and felt Its strength. The Darkness grew stronger; It consumed the Sisters and reached out to the cub's soul. The cub was too weak to resist, and as the Darkness absorbed the cub's soul, It laughed. "Now nothing will be safe!" roared the Darkness. "I have been waiting for this for centuries. Again, I have a physical form. Let Berryville beware!"

No longer were there two wolves running toward Berryville. There was only the Darkness. It had taken the form of a large, brown, ferocious she-wolf.

◆

CHAPTER 11 - WATER PARADE

Nerge, Kwingdale and Nerge's mother were down at Alfonses Lake watching the water parade opening ceremony. Field mice from all over the land came to enjoy the festivities. There were well over 1500 hundred mice in attendance. They ranged in age from infant mice to senior citizen mice. All were gathered to enjoy the water floats and the beginning of the Berry Festival.

As the floats neared the reviewing stand, where many of the mice were seated, a cry rang out from one of the mice who was seated near the top. "Look. A large wolf! Everyone run. She's heading straight toward us."

With these words there was wide spread fear and confusion. Quickly the stands emptied and mice began running in every direction. The mice on the water floats did not hear the alarm, and as the audience scattered wondered what was going on.

Remembering her dream, Nerge's mother said, "Don't run! Let's hide beneath this stand." Surprisingly neither Nerge nor Kwingdale argued.

And as the Darkness raced down the hill, the she-wolf began attacking the fleeing mice. Savagely It would catch a mouse by the throat, bite down and break its neck; then toss it away into the air. In all the years of Berryville, no one had witnessed a wolf attack. It was bloody and scores of mice lost their lives in a matter of minutes.

To avoid the she-wolf, many mice jumped into the Lake and tried to reach the water floats. Those who were on the floats helped the swimmers get out of the water.

It was a terrible sight. Anxiously, Nerge, Kwingdale and Nerge's mother crouched in fear below the reviewing stands, hoping the wolf would not see or smell them.

♦

Turtle glided along with the current and felt the water growing cold. Turtle realized the stream was feeding into a large body of water. His leg was feeling stronger so to increase speed he began to swim with the current.

After ten minutes, Turtle found himself in a large lake. The water was cool, clear and very deep. Swimming that short distance tired Turtle's leg and he decided to surface. Breaking the surface water, Turtle faced the high cliffs which surrounded Alfonses Lake. And as he marveled at their jagged beauty, he heard screaming and crying. Turning to see where this troubling sound came from, he beheld the confusion and carnage beside the grandstand. Swimming closer, he saw mice jumping into the water and being rescued. Next he saw a great, brown she-wolf attacking one mouse after another.

Turtle had never heard of a wolf attacking field mice; it simply did not happen. Then it occurred to Turtle, perhaps, he was there to help? That had been the point of the long journey. He arrived not to witness but to do something.

So Turtle began swimming toward shore. Although his leg still ached he fought past the pain and began to focus on the wolf. How could he stop the slaughter? Then it occurred to him, if he could somehow get the wolf in the water, there he had the advantage.

As Turtle neared shore he saw dead mice floating in the water and scattered on the hill. It was a shocking sight and Turtle got sick to his stomach. And as he grew sicker, he became indecisive and afraid. Should he continue? Perhaps it wasn't meant for him to interfere?

While Turtle hesitated in fear and indecision, the Riishi directed the Light. The Riishi had watched long enough; now it was time for action.

He projected a command to Turtle. This command was carried on the Light.

◆

"Pick up a sharpened stick!" This idea jumped into Turtle's mind. Turtle thought to himself, "I knew I would figure out what to do. I always get inspiration when I need it."

Cautiously Turtle climbed onto shore; he was careful not to be noticed by the she-wolf. Lying on the ground, beside the grandstand, were extra pieces of wood. They were part of the old seats and had been stacked by the builders. Turtle picked up a suitable piece, quickly sharpened the edge on a stone and prepared to do battle with the wolf.

◆

In the reviewing area, the Darkness killed or frightened away all the mice. Next, It turned toward the mice on the floats. Anxious to destroy everything in Berryville, the Darkness ran toward the water.

Standing in his way was a Turtle; the Darkness wondered, "What's a turtle doing here?" Without hesitation the Darkness raced toward Turtle and as she drew closer, Turtle raised his stick. The wolf just laughed at Turtle's effort to frighten. And as the wolf grabbed Turtle with her teeth, Turtle took the stick and jammed it deep into the she-wolf's right eye.

Suddenly, the wolf screamed in pain and dropped Turtle. Turtle was hurt and frightened and began to look for a place to hide. As Turtle crawled away, the she-wolf pulled the stick out of her eye. While one eye was bleeding, the other searched. Cursing, the Darkness vowed to make Turtle pay. Then the Darkness saw Turtle crawling toward the water and in a tremendous leap, the wolf jumped and grabbed Turtle. She lifted Turtle in her jaw and cracked Turtle's shell with her teeth. Then Turtle lost consciousness. Believing Turtle was dead, the she wolf tossed him far away into the Lake.

Slowly Turtle sank to the bottom of Alfonses Lake. Then the Riishi projected another command, "Awake! Awake!"

Somehow Turtle's unconscious mind sent a signal to Turtle's body and he awoke. Filled with pain and barely alive, Turtle lay at the bottom of the Lake. And as Turtle opened his eyes he saw a large, sparkling jewel. It was double his size and emanated a soft, healing white Light. Reaching out to touch the Light, Turtle felt stronger.

Wrapping his arms around the jewel, Turtle felt light as a feather. Then, Turtle began rising with the jewel from the bottom of the Lake.

In a matter of moments, the large sparkling jewel and Turtle were hovering above the water's surface. And as the jewel was in the sunlight, it picked up the sun's rays and began to reflect the Light across Berryville. In its brilliance, this ball of white pulsating Light consumed Turtle. And as the Darkness gazed upon the Light, It moaned in pain and suddenly vanished.

Growing brighter and brighter, the giant jewel flooded the whole region in beautiful, white Light, and then exploded. Some of the surviving mice ran to pick up jewel fragments, however, by the time they got to them, the fragments had turned into small, round, sparkling, white pebbles; which the mice quickly gathered up and placed in a large green urn.

◆

After witnessing the magnificence of the jewel and the destruction of the Darkness, Nerge and Kwingdale stepped out from beneath the grandstand. Nerge at once began to speak. It was an automatic thing. He didn't even think about what he was going to say. The words flowed as if they originated from another source.

"Citizens of Berryville, today the Light has vanquished the darkness. Although we have suffered many losses, we have also gained. Nothing can replace those who were lost but they are not dead. They live in splendor with the Great Mouse. He is author of what took place here today.

What has happened will be remembered for all time. Let us write it down and keep records of it. Let us never forget those who died so the Light might live."

Next, Kwingdale stood beside Nerge and spoke.

"There is much to do. Let us gather the fallen and bury them. Let us tend to the injured and establish a week of mourning. Then let us go about our lives. Let us establish a shrine of remembrance in our heart for each one who has fallen."

And as Nerge's mother listened she felt hope and a thought entered her heart. "No. The dead cannot be replaced but as the Great Mouse Wills, their lives can have meaning. We can remember how well they lived."

Then the surviving citizens of Berryville set about the task of tending to the injured, burying the fallen and reconstructing their lives.

♦

And as the sun began to set in Berryville, the mice were not alone. They were receiving help and guidance from a hidden friend.

Somewhere on a distant hill there was a Turtle whose job it was to reflect the Light to Berryville, Pond and the surrounding region. The Riishi had moved on to another realm. Turtle had taken the Riishi's place.

And as the years passed there was never a time when Berryville was without the Light or the guidance of a hidden friend.

♦

INTERPRETATIONS

Often we are quick to judge the impact of an event in a singular manner and look for the moral/meaning. In this story the rational mind is quick to say, "Good triumphs over evil" or "Never trust a devil in wolf's clothing." While these views may indeed be true, if we accept them as the only interpretation, we never go further.

In the story of Berryville, surely the Riishi viewed the events differently than the field mice that had relatives who died at the hands of the she-wolf. Also as the years go on different interpretations may be offered concerning who the turtle was and how he happened to be in Alfonses Lake. It is quite possible that schools of thought will develop concerning the various interpretations and field mice will receive awards for their essays on the subject.

For the spiritual traveler events are multidimensional. There is no one interpretation and to understand these various levels, events must be perceived holistically.

You may ask how I perceive something holistically. This view or ability is higher knowledge and represented in part by the jewel which Turtle found.

OTHER BOOKS BY STEWART BITKOFF

- *Journey of Light: Trilogy*, Authorhouse, 2004.

- *A Commuter's Guide to Enlightenment*, Llewellyn, 2008.

- *Sufism for Western Seekers*, Abandoned Ladder, 2011.

- *The Ferryman's Dream*, Abandoned Ladder, 2012.

- *Beyond The River's Gate*, Abandoned Ladder, 2014.

- *The Appleseed Journal*, Abandoned Ladder, 2014.

- *Light On The Mountain,* Abandoned Ladder, 2016

Books are available on **Amazon.com** in paperback and Kindle version.

ABOUT THE AUTHOR

Stewart Bitkoff grew up in New York City and spent most of his professional career living and working in the New York City area. An expert in therapeutic recreation and psychiatric rehabilitation and treatment, Dr. Bitkoff has been on the faculty or served as field instructor for multiple colleges and universities.

He has written work centering on the topic of the completed person and the original human development system. For years Dr. Bitkoff studied in two modern mystical schools. Professionally he worked to help the mentally ill integrate their altered states of consciousness into the physical world; recently he worked with children and their families as a behavioral consultant.

Please visit his website at http://www.stewartbitkoff.com or visit on **Facebook**.

www.ingramcontent.com/pod-product-compliance
Lightning Source LLC
LaVergne TN
LVHW051111080426
835510LV00018B/2001